Curriculum and the Life Erratic

TRANSGRESSIONS: CULTURAL STUDIES AND EDUCATION

Series Editor:
Shirley R. Steinberg, *University of Calgary, Canada*

Founding Editor:
Joe L. Kincheloe (1950–2008) *The Paulo and Nita Freire International Project for Critical Pedagogy*

Editorial Board

Jon Austin, *University of Southern Queensland, Australia*
Norman Denzin, *University of Illinois, Champaign-Urbana, USA*
Rhonda Hammer, *University of California Los Angeles, USA*
Nikos Metallinos, *Concordia University, Canada*
Christine Quail, *McMaster University, Canada*

This book series is dedicated to the radical love and actions of Paulo Freire, Jesus "Pato" Gomez, and Joe L. Kincheloe.

TRANSGRESSIONS: CULTURAL STUDIES AND EDUCATION

Cultural studies provides an analytical toolbox for both making sense of educational practice and extending the insights of educational professionals into their labors. In this context *Transgressions: Cultural Studies and Education* provides a collection of books in the domain that specify this assertion. Crafted for an audience of teachers, teacher educators, scholars and students of cultural studies and others interested in cultural studies and pedagogy, the series documents both the possibilities of and the controversies surrounding the intersection of cultural studies and education. The editors and the authors of this series do not assume that the interaction of cultural studies and education devalues other types of knowledge and analytical forms. Rather the intersection of these knowledge disciplines offers a rejuvenating, optimistic, and positive perspective on education and educational institutions. Some might describe its contribution as democratic, emancipatory, and transformative. The editors and authors maintain that cultural studies helps free educators from sterile, monolithic analyses that have for too long undermined efforts to think of educational practices by providing other words, new languages, and fresh metaphors. Operating in an interdisciplinary cosmos, Transgressions: Cultural Studies and Education is dedicated to exploring the ways cultural studies enhances the study and practice of education. With this in mind the series focuses in a non-exclusive way on popular culture as well as other dimensions of cultural studies including social theory, social justice and positionality, cultural dimensions of technological innovation, new media and media literacy, new forms of oppression emerging in an electronic hyperreality, and postcolonial global concerns. With these concerns in mind cultural studies scholars often argue that the realm of popular culture is the most powerful educational force in contemporary culture. Indeed, in the twenty-first century this pedagogical dynamic is sweeping through the entire world. Educators, they believe, must understand these emerging realities in order to gain an important voice in the pedagogical conversation.

Without an understanding of cultural pedagogy's (education that takes place outside of formal schooling) role in the shaping of individual identity--youth identity in particular--the role educators play in the lives of their students will continue to fade. Why do so many of our students feel that life is incomprehensible and devoid of meaning? What does it mean, teachers wonder, when young people are unable to describe their moods, their affective affiliation to the society around them. Meanings provided young people by mainstream institutions often do little to help them deal with their affective complexity, their difficulty negotiating the rift between meaning and affect. School knowledge and educational expectations seem as anachronistic as a ditto machine, not that learning ways of rational thought and making sense of the world are unimportant.

But school knowledge and educational expectations often have little to offer students about making sense of the way they feel, the way their affective lives are shaped. In no way do we argue that analysis of the production of youth in an electronic mediated world demands some "touchy-feely" educational superficiality.

What is needed in this context is a rigorous analysis of the interrelationship between pedagogy, popular culture, meaning making, and youth subjectivity. In an era marked by youth depression, violence, and suicide such insights become extremely important, even life saving. Pessimism about the future is the common sense of many contemporary youth with its concomitant feeling that no one can make a difference.

If affective production can be shaped to reflect these perspectives, then it can be reshaped to lay the groundwork for optimism, passionate commitment, and transformative educational and political activity. In these ways cultural studies adds a dimension to the work of education unfilled by any other sub-discipline. This is what Transgressions: Cultural Studies and Education seeks to produce—literature on these issues that makes a difference. It seeks to publish studies that help those who work with young people, those individuals involved in the disciplines that study children and youth, and young people themselves improve their lives in these bizarre times.

Curriculum and the Life Erratic

The Geographic Cure

Leslie B. Nissen

SENSE PUBLISHERS
ROTTERDAM/BOSTON/TAIPEI

A C.I.P. record for this book is available from the Library of Congress.

ISBN: 978-94-6209-360-7 (paperback)
ISBN: 978-94-6209-361-4 (hardback)
ISBN: 978-94-6209-362-1 (e-book)

Published by: Sense Publishers,
P.O. Box 21858,
3001 AW Rotterdam,
The Netherlands
https://www.sensepublishers.com/

Printed on acid-free paper

All Rights Reserved © 2013 Sense Publishers

No part of this work may be reproduced, stored in a retrieval system, or transmitted in any form or by any means, electronic, mechanical, photocopying, microfilming, recording or otherwise, without written permission from the Publisher, with the exception of any material supplied specifically for the purpose of being entered and executed on a computer system, for exclusive use by the purchaser of the work.

This book is dedicated to my brother, Geoffrey Burrell-Sahl.

Geoff, you were my navigator way before "that day with the map." From the minute you were born, you were the glue that kept me from falling apart. You may have been the younger one, but your wisdom trumped all. There I was, thinking I was protecting you, but you ended up shielding me many times over. You had an uncanny ability to defuse the thorniest of situations. You were the family compass, steering us around treacherous storms with your intuition, warmth, and wit. It was you who kept us all on an even keel. Thank you and I love you.

P.S. I still think you are the funniest guy on the planet.

TABLE OF CONTENTS

Acknowledgments	xi
1 Introduction: Curriculum and the Life Erratic	**1**
Inset: Stevie, Age Seven	1
The Geographic Cure, Curriculum Theory, and Psychoanalysis	3
A Matter of Balance	5
Wisdom Figures	12
The Singular Set of Children of Alcoholics	16
Overview of Chapters 2 through 6	19
2 The Confounded Life of an 80-Proof Home	**21**
Inset: Officer Jake's Steel-Toe Shoe	21
Retreats of Substance	23
Fermented Parenting	29
Taking Over	35
On Refusing to Talk About It	37
An Air Raid a Day	41
3 The Unhinged Lives of Kids on the Move	**47**
Inset: Ringo, Shut Up!	47
Families Unmoored	49
Transient Students Typically Defined	54
The Long, Loud Sigh: Student Mobility from the School Perspective	58
4 Drinking and Driving (Away)	**65**
Inset: Geography and His Sister	65
Glass Castles and Geography Lessons	67
The Buffer Has No Buffer	71
On The Fine Art of Cigarette Removal	73
Secrets and Lies, Good Moods and Goodbyes	76
Whispers in the Roar	80
Driving Away	83
5 "Hold Still"	**85**
Inset: The Laundrymat Lizard	85
Charlie's Angel and Mystical Whispers	87
The Ken Factor	92
The Golden Option	99
Naming It, Claiming It	101
The Doctor, The Cape, and the Red Letter "S"	103

TABLE OF CONTENTS

    Forget-Me-Nots and Contradictory Spaces   106
    So, We Were STUCK In This Plastic, Outdoor Elevator . . .   110
    Holding Chaos at Bay   114

6 The Geographic Cure Writ Large   **119**
    Inset: Stevie, Age 12   123

References   125

ACKNOWLEDGMENTS

I extend my most heartfelt gratitude to the following professors in Georgia Southern University's Curriculum Studies Program. They are:

- Dr. Marla Morris, a scholar to the core, my academic mentor, who taught me how to think psychoanalytically, read critically, write autobiographically, and trust my own voice.
- Dr. John Weaver, whose classes in cultural studies were not just eye opening, but foundation shaking, and whose insights always proved to be invaluable.
- Dr. Daniel Chapman, who helped me carve coherent thoughts out of a block of indistinct deliberations, and who prodded me to "complicate" those thoughts beyond my comfort zone.

I am also very grateful to Dr. Mary Aswell Doll of the Savannah College of Art and Design, an exceptionally creative teacher and writer, who taught me about "wisdom figures" by being an incomparable one herself.

Two additional professors in GSU's Curriculum Studies Program must be thanked as well: Dr. Ming Fang He, whose enthusiastic commitment to this field left a lasting impression on me, and Dr. William Reynolds, who opened my eyes by challenging what I *thought* I knew about educational policy.

Additionally, I am indebted to Dr. Michael Keith of Boston College (author of *The Next Better Place*) for graciously meeting with me a few years ago, and allowing me to pester him with questions as we compared notes about our childhoods. Mike: I'm proud to now call you my friend, and proud that we are both survivors in more ways than one.

I am thankful for Erin Martineau, formatting expert and proofreading guru, for her amazing professional expertise, and I am grateful to Sense publishers Peter de Liefde and Michele Lokhorst, as well as Sense *Transgressions* series editor Shirley Steinberg, for supporting this endeavor.

Thank you to the following friends who had a HUGE impact on this project:

- Debbie Burnette, my doctoral program ally / think tank colleague / partner in crime / paper reviewer / and movies-trump-work buddy, for being there with me this whole time. Thanks also for taking one for the team; your wild goose chase for "the Bergamo video" remains a classic.
- Melodie Moore, for keeping me together when I was descending into *Perrla-Deleted-My-References Hell* while I was trying to wrap this baby up. Thank you also for being the first to read all the chapters in order, back to back, and for providing essential input.
- Heather Bilton, for not hating me when I "left" you (job-wise) in order to go back to work in a school, thinking I could more easily work on this book that

ACKNOWLEDGMENTS

- way. I know; I was delusional. You didn't hold a grudge (for long) and remained a faithful supporter.
- Julie Gannam, because, if not for you, there would be no "finished" book; there would be no *me* at all. Thank you also for understanding that recovery takes forever.
- Dearest, dearest Jennie, thank you for saying "yes." I would never have told the whole story in Chapter 5 without your blessing. Your courage is phenomenal.

More friends and colleagues must be thanked for supporting me in countless ways during my journey through these chapters, and through life: Syril Barnes, Angela Bohne, Amber Crump, Cindy Clifton, Domenica Devine, Julie Diebolt, Charlene Harrell, Carol Hendry, Grace Herrington, Charlene Jones, Katherine Johnson, Judy Newsome, Linda Oliver, Gayle Powers, Kathy Roux, Ruth Sales, Kim Sancomb, Sherrie Sauer, John Sutlive, and Rose Talbert (a.k.a "Miss Wose Tabbitt"). If I left out a name, please forgive me. I can still claim chemo brain for a while longer.

A grateful hug goes to Erin Tova Mullins, the young artist whose drawing was commissioned a few years ago for the cover of this book. Erin is older now, and is quite the budding actress. Remember her name.

If every single star in the galaxy blinked "thank you" in the night sky, their messages would still not adequately convey my gratitude to my family. I owe so much to:

- David Smith, Rebecca and Michael Panarisi and kids, Jason and Jennifer Smith and kids, plus my *de facto* siblings Debbie Fischer, Kathy Godfrey, and Michael Teasley, for putting up with books and papers all over the dining room when you visited us, and/or for tolerating my constant references to *working on the book* when we talked on the phone or visited. Thank you so much for not yelling "enough, already!" More importantly, thank you for caring.
- Monica Sippel, my heart sister (forget "ex"—forget "step"): I love you for listening, and for understanding why I had to *go there*. You genuinely understand the Life Erratic.
- Marlene Burrell-Sahl, my wonderful sister-in-law, for seeing my brother as the treasure that he is, and for creating for him the *happily ever after* that he has deserved for so long. *You* are a treasure as well.

Thank you Colleen Nissen, my beautiful and amazingly gifted stepdaughter, for being genuinely interested in my ideas for this book early on, and for encouraging me from beginning to end. Thank you for helping me categorize my bazillion references (when we were herding cats), for typing from many of those references, and *especially* for never thinking that I was too old or feeble-minded to be a graduate student. You totally rock. Also, I want *your* job when I grow up.

Thank you Sam Prevatt, my brilliant, generous-hearted son, for your exceptional proofreading eye, your suggestions, and your astute questions, all of which helped to make this book better than it ever would have been otherwise. The phrase, "I could never have done it without you," never rang more true than in regard to you. Thank you for your time, your input, and your gentle, get-on-with-it-already reminder that Papa would be proud of me. Thank you also for popping the question to Amy, the only woman on earth whom I would ever consider a perfect match for my son.

Thank you, Andreas Nissen, my husband and the love of my life. This expedition would never have been completed if not for your belief in me. You never doubted that I could meet the next task at hand, even when I had doubts. Thank you for meeting me at the diner late at night after class, and for understanding why my nose was always in a book at home. Thank you for letting me leave you notes that said, "Will you wake me up when you get up?" when I was trying to finish a paper. When cancer threw a monkey wrench into the mix, thank you for being willing to "run off" with me, and for being my caregiver—the hardest job in the world. Thank you for enduring the constant stream of "Helga matters" that I had to contend with, when Alzheimer's disease consumed our lives and stole hers. When I was finally ready to *put up or shut up*, thank you for tolerating my need to (again) turn the whole house into my personal workspace. You made all the difference in the world, because you were always in my corner, every step of the way. I am forever grateful *to* you, and grateful to God *for* you.

CHAPTER 1

INTRODUCTION: CURRICULUM AND THE LIFE ERRATIC

There are people who can be defined by what they escape from, and people who are defined by the fact that they are forever escaping.
—Adam Phillips, *Houdini's Box: The Art of Escape*

INSET: STEVIE, AGE SEVEN

In the middle of a muggy, late October morning, a small, shy, second-grade boy named Stevie is called out of his class by Ms. Jones, a school administrator whom Stevie doesn't know. Ms. Jones tells the child, "Don't worry, you're not in trouble. I just need to talk to you about something. Come walk with me." Rain starts to fall as they walk through the breezeway between wings; they're headed for the front office. Ms. Jones tries to make small talk about southeast Georgia's version of fall weather, attempting to put the child at ease. Stevie does not respond. He pulls his cold little fingers away from her clammy hand as they walk. When they get to her office, Ms. Jones sits with Stevie at a conference table and picks up a large brown file folder full of papers. "Steven, we had quite a time trying to locate your school records! Goodness, you've moved around a bit, haven't you?" She plasters a big smile across her face. There is lead in the air, upstaging the humidity.

The administrator presses on. "When your mother came to register you here at the beginning of the year, we put you in Miss Lacey's class because she had the fewest number of students. But it looks like you need more help in math than she can give you." Stevie's facial expression changes from confusion to fear. The little color he had in his face drains away.

"Your records are finally here," Ms. Jones says, "and we see that you had special math help last year at one of the schools you attended. I think you will be better off in Mr. Caison's class. Wouldn't you like to be one of his Terrific Tigers?" The woman's forced cheerfulness makes the seven-year-old wince. His mom uses that kind of voice when she announces where the family will move next, or what her new job will involve. Stevie's big brother, Josh, calls it *Mom's Fake Happy Voice*, which, Josh explains, is quite different from *Mom's Pissy Drunk Voice*.

Waterfalls tumble down Stevie's cheeks. His head bows down in acute grief. The only time the little boy speaks during this entire session is when he murmurs, "Do I have to?" The woman's lightning-bolt "Yes!" slashes through his heart. As Ms. Jones steers Stevie back across the breezeway to the first-grade wing, she chatters on about

CHAPTER 1

how much he'll like Mr. Caison's class. Tears continue to roll, to the point that the child can barely see to walk. When they get to Miss Lacey's door, Stevie wraps his arms around his teacher's legs, and sobs. Certainly, the teacher's unfailingly calm and nurturing demeanor has been a balm to his frenzied soul. But there's more. Stevie's teacher of five weeks has been the first stabilizing influence that the boy has known. The little routines that Miss Lacey puts into place during their school day offer a world of comfort for him. Consistency is an urgent, unmet need for Stevie, the Child of an Alcoholic. He craves something that he cannot even articulate. Haugland (2005) explains:

> Predictability allows the person to prepare for what is coming and then, when it is safe, he/she can relax. Children have a limited ability to understand parental alcohol abuse and to predict changes occurring in family rituals and routines because of the drinking. (p. 238)

Stevie has never understood the continual upheaval going on in his life. However, it was beginning to look as though there might be many more happy days ahead with Miss Lacey. Josh, wiser at 13 and quite adept at reading all the signs, had been speculating that their mother "might actually stick to this job for a while."

However, Ms. Jones wants Stevie in a smaller class with more opportunities for math remediation. As a school administrator she has worked tirelessly to boost the school's math scores on mandated district and state tests. "Placing children with the right teacher is critical," Ms. Jones pontificates in staff meetings. "Even in the lower grades, this is a high-stakes situation!" Indeed. The two-edged sword of "high stakes" cuts deep and wide. Teachers at Ms. Jones's school believe that she doesn't "get it," but she actually does. It's just that she has chosen the hill on which she's prepared to die. There is unrelenting pressure from Ms. Jones's superiors demanding that she get her school taken off the state's "Needs Improvement" list. Her paycheck is generated in the world of the public school, described so aptly by Parks (1999) as "a place that today, ironically, remains among those most marred by rigidity and the hopelessly misguided cult of efficiency" (p. 272). And now that she sees the dismal report in Stevie's records regarding his math performance, she has to act.

Ms. Jones directs Stevie, a bit too crisply, to retrieve his belongings out of his cubby. Miss Lacey tries unsuccessfully to blink back her own tears. The other children in the room are silent and sad. Miss Lacey whispers reassurances to Stevie as she tries to peel the boy away from her. Ms. Jones has had it with the tears and the melodrama. *The child and this teacher both need to suck it up and get on with it.* "Steven, come on. Be a big boy. Mr. Caison is waiting." She ends up grabbing the pint-sized book bag herself, and tugs at the boy's arm to haul him away. And here—right here where this scene is freeze-framed—is the central core of this book: the destructive manner in which the alcoholic parent's quest for the Geographic Cure impacts school-aged Children of Alcoholics, and the systemic inadequacies that I see in education's response to their needs.

INTRODUCTION: CURRICULUM AND THE LIFE ERRATIC

THE GEOGRAPHIC CURE, CURRICULUM THEORY, AND PSYCHOANALYSIS

> A young girl strokes the tight braids
> of her hair and thinks she is one memory.
> —Tess Galagher, *Moon Crossing Bridge*

Stevie's mother Kay, a twice-divorced mother of three, is overwhelmed with troubles that consume her thoughts and fill her glass. When the going gets tough, Kay gets going . . . out of the neighborhood, out of the workplace, out of the life of the latest boyfriend, or all of the above. Alcoholics Anonymous (AA) defines this response to life's problems as the "Geographic Cure"—the repeated attempts of an alcoholic to cure his/her alcoholism with a new beginning (Alcoholics Anonymous [AA], n.d., p. 1). When a drinker on the run is a parent, there are often devastating ramifications for the child. Growing up in the midst of endless change means living with chronic inconsistency, insecurity, and fear. That upbringing—with its inherent vicious cycle of life-altering changes—creates a host of problems for the Children of Alcoholics who are pulled along on the chase. Children of Alcoholics and the Geographic Cure are the subjects of this book; therefore, I choose not to use the familiar "COA" abbreviation, but to spell out the term instead. I spell out the term "Geographic Cure" with each use as well, as I do with other terminology that will appear soon. As a small show of respect for the children who live this life, I recognize the encumbrance of these terms, rather than fly past them. (Abbreviations do appear when they are part of direct quotations.)

The literal version of the Geographic Cure for Children of Alcoholics means being the perennial new kid, who, despite new living quarters, still has the old burdens on his back. Many times there is no second parent around to deflect the emotional (and sometimes physical) blows. As is also typical for Children of Alcoholics, the child has to "cover" for and "parent" the parent, take care of siblings, and make the best of each situation. The Geographic Cure adds another load to the already weighty burden of the Child of an Alcoholic: dealing with life on top of a sinkhole. Making the best of the situation means dealing with *new* situations, endlessly. New state, new city (or just a new apartment three blocks over), new relative to encroach upon . . . regardless of the particulars, the Geographic Cure means there is always a run toward the *new*, or at least, the *different from this*. The children in tow have to continually scramble to keep up, in every respect. The psychological impact of this life upon such children is profound, as is the lack of awareness on the part of many adults who encounter them.

Even if the physical address does not change, the figurative version of this search for a cure is the alcoholic's sprint toward every new-and-improved plan that pops in his or her head. The alcoholic is sure that a fresh start is all that's needed, and *then* he or she will stop drinking, once life is better. "When entire families organize themselves around the behavior of an alcoholic, individuals are continually kept off balance while anticipating drinking behaviors that are entirely unpredictable"

CHAPTER 1

(O'Rourke, 1990, December, p. 3). The alcoholic often changes jobs or starts and stops working frequently. She continually seeks out new friends, new lovers, new interests. If she's a parent, she offers little stability to her children, if any. The only certainty that the Child of an Alcoholic can depend upon is that the parent will change horses mid-stream. Flimsy attempts at permanence melt away like ice cubes. Structure dissolves. Children under the care of these parents have no idea what the next day, even the next hour, will bring. An alcoholic mother very often mirrors one of the "borderline mothers" described by Christina Lawson (2004), who writes,

> "Now" is all that matters to borderlines. Laura's mother could spank and scold her one minute and hug her next. One time she threatened to get rid of her, packed her suitcase, and later the same day told her she couldn't live without her. (p. 27)

The ground shifts beneath Children of Alcoholics at every turn. Despite the fact that, as Alice Miller (1990) notes, children need "the respect and protection of adults who take them seriously, love them, and honestly help them to become oriented to the world" (p. 167), little protection is offered to many Children of Alcoholics. Their orientation to the world is skewed. Emotional distress increases each time another family relocation is added to the mix.

Within the Children of Alcoholics population, the faction whom I have named "Geographic Cure Children" comprises a school-aged group who grow up with an alcoholic pulling them wherever the grass is greener. When frequent moves are the norm, such kids are often viewed in schools as "highly mobile" children, but there is much more to the story than transiency alone. They are confused, traumatized children who pocket many terrifying secrets before opening their front door to face the world. While this study devotes some attention to the distressing life of a child who endures a chronically drunk parent at *home*, my particular focus is on how that dilemma weighs heavily upon the child at *school*. Considering that, for nearly 10 months of every year of their K-12 lives, students spend more waking hours at school than they do at home, educators are the adults most likely to help Geographic Cure Children make sense of the world. For this reason, the consideration of Geographic Cure Children *as students* dominates my writing. Children who are surviving a chronically unpredictable life with an alcoholic parent are often as neglected in school as they are at home. The standards-driven, "all of us on the same page," high-stakes freak-out design of schooling in the 21st century means that the teacher who encounters this child has little time, if any, to explore what she might intuitively feel: The new kid with a permanent record as long as a '57 Oldsmobile is a *special needs* child in the most vital sense.

My primary objective is to bring to curriculum studies a new thread of conversation that I have not seen explored within the field: the far-reaching impact of the Geographic Cure, and the understanding of curriculum as *erratic* text. Inherent in this study are implications for educators, education professors, counselors,

INTRODUCTION: CURRICULUM AND THE LIFE ERRATIC

nurses, school social workers, and others who work with Children of Alcoholics. It is important, I think, to start this dialogue within the field of curriculum studies, where, as explained by Pinar, Reynolds, Slattery, and Taubman (2002), the emphasis is on *understanding*, rather than developing, curriculum. In the tradition of the curriculum scholars from whom I've learned so much, I hope to encourage educators and community members alike to, as Pinar et al. (2002) phrase it, "reflect more profoundly" (p. 9) and consider what it might mean to work with highly mobile, highly fragile children.

My interest in this area took shape as I worked through the "infinitive form of curriculum" known as *currere* (Pinar, 2004, p. 4). This study is the result of my own *currere:* remembering my own Geographic Cure childhood, and imagining a future in which I begin a complicated conversation (playing on Wes Anderson's (2004) movie title, *The Life Aquatic with Steve Zissou*) about what I've termed "the Life Erratic." In doing so, I gain a deeper understanding of my "submergence in the present," where I am finding myself mobilized to speak out (Pinar et al., 2002, pp. 4–5). My study is not, however, about proposing new "methods" or "best practices" to address the issues. As John Weaver (2002) points out, methods can "stifle possibilities, even when they are meant to enlighten. This is one of the flaws of the Western world. We covet method and dismiss humans" (p. 169). I chose instead the path of theoretical research rather than suggesting practical curricular choices. Curriculum research involves deepening the knowledge that is pertinent to the making of such choices. I hope to add to that understanding in order to encourage *relevant* choices in schools. To my knowledge, the impact of the Geographic Cure upon Children of Alcoholics has not been explored in the curriculum studies field. I feel quite fortunate to be able to bring Geographic Cure Children into the light in this field, where there are scholars who care about the child-as-human, as opposed to the child-as-test-score. The issue is widespread, timely, and urgently in need of exploration. There are numerous Geographic Cure Children, like Stevie, in schools *now*, whose alcoholic parents continually pull the rug out from under them. The numbers (which I address later in this chapter) seem to be climbing every year.

A MATTER OF BALANCE

> The great thing in all education is to make our nervous system our ally instead of our enemy.
> —William James, *Talks to Teachers on Psychology; And to Students on Some of Life's Ideals*

For me, psychoanalysis is the lens through which the Geographic Cure can best be explored. Psychoanalysis blends well with curriculum theory; they have been fused together for decades. As far back as 1935, Anna Freud spoke about this unification while delivering a series of lectures to an audience of teachers in Vienna. She explained what psychoanalysis does for pedagogy, including providing "a criticism of existing educational methods," broadening "the teacher's knowledge of human beings," and honing the teacher's "understanding of the complicated relations between the child and the educator" (A. Freud, 1936/1961, p. 106). The relationship between child and teacher would certainly be more meaningful if the teacher understood more about what motivates human actions and reactions to others.

Louise Tyler, wife of Ralph Tyler (who created the "Tyler Rationale"), also illuminated the pedagogical benefits of blending the two fields. This is surprising, since her husband's work was "the model for the entire behavioral objectives approach that has dominated public school curriculum over the last forty years" (Pagano, 2004, p. 95). Ralph Tyler (1969) equated curriculum with linear steps, measureable goals, and specific evaluation procedures. In 1958, however, Louise Tyler published an article titled, "Psychoanalysis and Curriculum," in which she stated that "curriculum theory, which is basically and primarily concerned with man and his nature, could profit from an application of some of the most significant insights that have been developed about man" (p. 447). She explained that teachers need to understand transference, because it would be "helpful if the teacher knows that [a student's] first reactions are not under his control and that he is not responsible for them" (p. 456). Tyler used this example as part of her larger point, which was that, in education, "the concepts of the unconscious, of man's instinctual nature . . . will be of service. These concepts may not provide solutions, but they may change our understanding of the educative process—if only to deepen our understanding of its complexity" (p. 456).

Several decades later, when Pinar and Grumet (2006) encouraged curriculum scholars to bring in fresh perspectives from outside of education, they included psychoanalysis as one of the fields to be considered. They referred to psychoanalysis as "the bridge between the arts and sciences," because that particular discipline "combines the specificity and symbolic ambiguity of literature with the generalities and recurring patterns of the social sciences" (p. 112). Marla Morris (2006) explains: "Curriculum theorizing and psychoanalysis are natural bedfellows because both deal with the psyche and the world of the child" (pp. 125–126). Psychoanalytic thinking can contribute to the consideration of education as a process conducted *between teacher and student* rather than imparted *by teacher to student.* Deborah Britzman and Alice Pitt (1996) speak from a psychoanalytic perspective when calling for teachers to learn from their students' learning. They recall Anna Freud's investigation of learning itself, which "begins with a central concept in psychoanalysis, that of 'transference,' or the idea that one's past unresolved conflicts with others and within the self are projected onto the meanings of new interactions" (Britzman & Pitt, 1996, p. 117). When considering the connections between transference and pedagogy, I am particularly interested in the ways in which teachers respond to children who come into the classroom mid-year, interrupting the existing classroom "vibe." "Indeed," Britzman and Pitt continue, "recent writing about pedagogy suggests that transference shapes how teachers respond and listen to students, and how students respond and listen to teachers" (p. 117).

In describing the purpose of psychoanalysis, Adam Phillips (2001b) uses language that echoes Pinar's explanation of *currere*:

> Psychoanalysis, Lacan writes in his Ecrits, "is a question of recollection . . . in which conjectures about the past are balanced against promises of the future." In this balancing act, to be remembering is to be planning a future. And to call up the future is the project of psychoanalysis. (p. 375)

For conjectures about the past to be made, however, we sometimes have to take trips down some dark, scary memory lanes. For me, there is much still buried in the bushes along those lanes. I still hesitate sometimes to "go there," especially when the road circles back to family and memories that seem better left under cover. Morris (2001) articulates this feeling precisely:

> Memory gets stuck; it becomes lodged in the heart of the psyche. Repressed memory is located somewhere between the remembered and the forgotten; it becomes haunting and torments survivors because it never goes away. Repressed memory somehow gets intraphysically passed down to the next generation. (p. 37)

I learned much about transgenerational trauma from Marla Morris during my doctoral studies. When I was young I cared little about how my mother "Marcia" grew up, even less about how *her* mother grew up. But now I'm interested in my grandmother's stifled Cherokee heritage, my grandfather's fondness for a nip, and my mother's appearance on the scene as a "change-of-life baby." Their experiences have woven themselves into my understanding of an alcoholic mother and her melancholia. Drinking was the only remedy my mother knew. McDougall (1985) writes about Sophie, a woman much like my mother, whose alcoholism was "an attempt to take flight from intolerable affective states of anger and abandonment that she could neither contain nor elaborate. She had little tolerance for the mental pain caused by strong negative feelings" (p. 87). That is an apt description of Marcia, and, I would venture, many other alcoholics as well. Feelings of rage and abandonment encircled my mother's life from the moment she came into the world as an unwanted baby. Those feelings framed her relationships with alcohol, and with my brother and me from the time each of us were born. Like her mother before her, Marcia did not meet Winnicott's (1989b) criteria for a "good enough mother":

> What is needed . . . by the infant is not some kind of perfection of mothering, but a good enough adaptation, that which is part of a living partnership in which the mother temporarily identifies herself with her infant. To be able to identify herself with her infant to the necessary degree, the mother needs to be protected from external reality so that she may enjoy a period of preoccupation, the baby being the object of her preoccupation. (p. 44)

Unfortunately, where excessive drinking abounds, external reality seeps into the fold each time a new bottle is opened; the infant's position as the mother's top preoccupation is usurped. My father was around when I was an infant, and I was shielded somewhat from Marcia's depression and pain for nearly four years. However, my dad divorced my mother twice; their remarriage "for the sake of the child" could not be sustained. In the 1960s, judges hearing custody cases most often sided with the mother, and both court battles were no exception. Not realizing that she was pregnant with my brother Geoffrey, my mother signed divorce papers in Washington, D.C. and made a plan to haul me across the country to California. Marcia's subsequent discovery of her pregnancy did not alter that plan. When my brother arrived a few months after we moved, no father was there to offset, for him, our mother's depression. There was just an eight-year-old sister who tried to take on the role of buffer.

Via memory work, I make my conjectures about my past. And I can begin to see the bigger picture of how my early life experiences affect my relations with others. Psychoanalytic thinking is a critical piece of the puzzle that is *currere*: "Curriculum conceived as *currere* requires not only the study of autobiography, history, and social theory, it requires as well the serious study of psychoanalytic theory" (Pinar, 2004, p. 57). I have strong feelings about the usefulness of such study—I wish that some level of psychoanalytic theory could be required of both pre-service teachers and educators pursuing advanced degrees. However, as Pinar (2004) notes, within the field there is a history of "interest" in psychoanalysis, but that interest was largely squelched "as business thinking and political interests dominated the school curriculum" (p. 57). Yes, of course—the *business* model for schooling. I know it well, since I worked in a public school in Georgia, a state that wholeheartedly embraces that model. As I see it, this move toward business principles contributes to what Christopher Lasch (1979) calls the "Atrophy of Competence":

> Sweeping social changes, reflected in academic practice, thus underlie the deterioration of the school system and the consequent spread of stupidity. . . . Standards of teaching decline, the victims of poor teaching come to share the experts' low opinion of their capacities, and the teaching profession complains of unteachable students. (pp. 127–128)

Highly mobile children are, indeed, often considered by teachers to be "unteachable." This is why it's important to think psychoanalytically, as Morris (2006) describes: "Thinking psychoanalytically means thinking in terms of relation-to-other. The ways in which one thinks about the other can alter the ways in which one thinks about the self" (p. 72). In my experience, the only consideration of *self* that is encouraged in most public school arenas is in regard to the question: "How am I doing with standards and test scores?"

Thinking psychoanalytically within a school setting does not mean that the teacher assumes the role of analyst. However, Parsons (2000) tells of one intriguing viewpoint regarding therapy that I think could also apply, in part, to pedagogical relationships. Describing therapy as "a symmetrical encounter between two individuals," Parsons adds, "although the focus is on helping one of them, this does not mean the other has to be a different, special sort of person" (p. 11). Parsons writes that therapy (and, I would add, *teaching*) "depends on ordinary human qualities like warmth, tact and emotional sensitivity, and the therapist is simply someone with experience" who is trying to help someone else (p. 11). Teachers who can convey genuine warmth and concern for students stand a better chance of initiating and sustaining the complicated conversations about violence, marginalization, and hate that need to take place in classrooms, as well as discussions about drugs and their impact on families.

The notion of *care* seems to be absent in the current wave of school improvement efforts, which hammer down so hard on teachers that they literally don't have time to build relationships. Cloninger (2008) asks:

> [H]ow does the teacher's internal state affect the culture in the classroom? What would a culture in the classroom look like if the teacher focused on loving students? The obvious and recurrent criticism regarding the role of love and empathy in the classroom is that such ideas are "touchy-feely," "soft," or "overly-sensitive." Indeed the criticism is not only misguided but naïve, for it is precisely such an approach that is missing from so many learning environments across the country. (p. 196)

Educators rarely have the luxury of time on their side, with the pressures to keep up with every new initiative, strategy, and requirement (such as staying on the same page as their grade or subject-level colleagues). Therefore, it is incredibly difficult to focus on loving their students. States and school districts will not leave teachers alone for a minute. They keep "tinkering," with the curriculum, as Noddings (1992, p. 3) describes. It's the "tinkering" that drives teachers crazy, because not a year goes by without the implementation of another set of new initiatives. Workshops and trainings abound, drilling the newest objectives, standards, pacing guides, and discipline strategies into teachers' skulls. Every year!

I agree with Noddings' (1992) contention that the primary goal of schools should be to "promote the growth of students as healthy, competent, moral people.... We cannot ignore our children—their purposes, anxieties, and relationships—in the service of making them more competent in academic skills" (p. 10). For those Geographic Cure Children whose anxieties are well hidden, healthy growth and academic competency are not always visible on the horizon. If only there were time in the day to foster a sense of community in the classroom, and to help children learn how to care, and to be cared for. What really happens is that if it's not one person tinkering with the curriculum, it's another—or rather, countless others. Everyone is searching for The Next Big Thing in education, and, in the midst of it all, the child disappears. It's defeating enough for a Child of an Alcoholic to find a profound absence of caring at home, yet schools are often just as devoid of care. Children should not have to "earn" care, but in many cases that's exactly what happens. David Purpel (2003) lays out this fact starkly:

> Schools are one of those places where dignity is rationed and affirmation has to be earned every day, where students have to struggle to be accepted and

valued, and where teachers and administrators dole out varying degrees of love, acceptance, and approval. Underneath all these negotiations and transactions is the fundamental message, however unspoken, that some people are better than others and that it is proper to devise ways to determine who is better and what the consequences are to be. (p. x)

No child should have to struggle to be accepted by teachers. Often struggling for *any* kind of positive connection at home, kids should find a safe haven in schools, where love and acceptance should abound. The real story, of course, is that *compassion* is an abstract word on the "character trait of the month" list. If kids who attend the same school all year have a tough time struggling for acceptance, imagine the uphill battle ahead of the child who arrives at his or her third school of the year.

Rebecca Martusewicz (2001) puts forth an image that sticks with me: "We can only move toward the good by recognizing and being awake to suffering, by leaning into it, and this requires considering others' needs" (p. 106). This book is ultimately a call to action for educators to *lean into* and meaningfully reflect on the anguish of transient children whose only constant is that a parent gets drunk every night. School may well be the only venue where a child in distress might be nurtured. Ted Aoki (2005) uses the term "nurture" in many of his essays, while writing about trusting our instincts, insights, and intuition, telling us that "a truly educated person speaks and acts from a deep sense of humility," and that "to be educated is to be ever open to the call of what it is to be deeply human, and heeding the call to walk with others in life's ventures" (p. 365). If such truly educated people were the policy makers in education, maybe we'd finally see the notion of *care* taken seriously.

When children are not cared for, they also are not learning how to care. None of us who teach children, or who prepare others to do so, should assume that all children learn to care at home. Thomas Cottle (2004) writes,

> Some children . . . are not exposed to the love curriculum. They never know about love. These are the psychological if not literal latchkey children, the ones home alone even when all sorts of people may be around. (p. 46)

I am quite ashamed to admit that decades ago I was one of those teachers who insisted that whatever was going on at home should be *checked at the door.* It took a couple of years before I came to fully understand that there were kids sitting in my classes who, at home, were devalued at best—or worse, truly unloved. Those problems cannot be neatly tucked away before the school day begins. Yet when I was first employed as a teacher, my position was that my students were not to even think about utilizing *problems at home* as an excuse for anything, whether implicitly or outright. After a while it finally dawned on me that I was teaching the way I was taught, with only a very few exceptions. I was expecting of those children what was expected of me, forgetting all about the part where leaving problems at the door was impossible.

INTRODUCTION: CURRICULUM AND THE LIFE ERRATIC

I've been on both sides of the street: first as a Geographic Cure Child, and then as a teacher who had to "deal with" transient children. This is why, as part of the process of *currere*, I employ an autobiographical slant in this book. I can best anchor a theoretical exploration of the Geographic Cure in, as Mary Doll (2000) phrases it, "curriculum's connection to lived experience" (p. xiii). During my doctoral program, I realized that in fact I could only write effectively about a topic that seeped out of my pores. Autobiography is at the core of *currere*; self-knowledge is enhanced by autobiographical writing. Paula Salvio (2006), who extensively studied the life and mental illness of poet and teacher Ann Sexton, discusses Sexton's narratives in which she recalled teaching college students about her particular writing process. Salvio puts forward the idea that Sexton's pedagogical narratives about writing "combine to form a narrative of reparation that is used to recognize and work through ambivalent relationships with the lost object, in this case a 'safe and secure home'" (p. 84). Such is the "lost object" for children of the Geographic Cure—there is little in their childhoods that would be synonymous with *safe and secure*. Salvio adds, "In exploring the possibility of reparation in writing and teaching, I consider the project of cultivating a 'true self,' for women who, like Sexton, have experienced . . . subtle, 'as yet unnamed' traumas" (p. 67). I grew up in a cloud of traumas, some named, some most assuredly not named, and even though I'm 58 years old, it seems to me that my "true self" is still germinating.

When I was young I secretly wrote in a diary, on a regular basis, about trauma in my life. My plan was to have an account, on paper, of what my existence was like, so that when I became a parent, I would remember how *not* to behave. However, there is much more to the process of *currere* than naming the hurt. Pinar et al. (2002) state, "Autobiography is considerably more than the 'interpretation of lived experience' . . . [it] is inextricably social and political" (p. 546). During those teen years, my expectation was that once I became an adult, I would get over the humiliating aspects of my story and tell the world what it was like to live a transitory life driven by alcohol-soaked decisions made on the fly. It seems to me now that my topic found me while I was writing in that diary. Pinar and Grumet (2006) state:

> The autobiographical stories that *currere* tells appear in the first narration to bear the quality of truth; after all, they are the subject's own statement about his experience. In the telling the subject gains some active mastery over what he may have experienced passively, an impulse Freud recognized common both to child's play and to the artist's creativity. The purpose of these stories is not, however, to lull the narrator and his audience into the neat resolution of happy endings. . . . Once the entries are recorded, they are read to reveal what other actions, responses, or interpretations might have been available to the narrator. (pp. 133–134)

As an adult, to look at what else might have been done or said is to be reflective and critical at the same time. There were a few years of woefully inept teaching behind me before I learned from an older teacher the benefits of reflection. Now,

CHAPTER 1

when I mentor new teachers, I encourage reflective thinking *and writing*. It startles them, however, when I tell them I don't need to see their reflections. I just want to inspire the process of looking back in order to look ahead. Madeleine Grumet (2004) explains why this is so critical: "The teacher who can be the critic of her own assumptions can welcome the diversity of her students' experiences without defensiveness and denial" (p. 243). I urgently wish that in schools there would be far more recognition and welcoming of transient students' experiences, and far less thinly masked exasperation at having to "deal" with a new child mid-year. For that to happen, teachers would need to be willing to truthfully reflect upon their own feelings about what it means to embrace the child who disrupts the "community of the classroom." What an eye-opener it was for me to realize, early in my teaching career, that I was transferring all of my baggage about *being* the new kid years ago to the *actual* new kids who were brought to me in December, or, even worse, March.

Patrick Slattery (2006) remarks that as he works with pre-service teachers, he reflects upon his own (Tyler-dominated) undergraduate teacher training. Slattery explains that he continually calls to mind his own past experiences as he chooses textbooks, plans learning experiences, and decides what films to show and which guest speakers to invite. Looking back, looking inward, before moving forward and outward, is *currere*. Without question, my life under the influence of the Geographic Cure shapes who I am. However, what drives this project is the fact that I often recognized the impact of that Cure on children during the 28 years that I taught in the public school system. And while my research has shown me that problems related to highly mobile or transient students are gaining more and more attention as topical, global issues, the connection between student mobility and parental alcoholism is only rarely recognized.

WISDOM FIGURES

> Fire ants had taken over the yard; their venomous mounds were like land mines, and we were careful to dodge them. The gun was never found. Daddy must have hidden it after the fight. We were looking for something that wasn't there—and running from what was. Just like Mama and Daddy.
> —Lauretta Hannon, *The Cracker Queen: A Memoir of a Jagged, Joyful Life*

> The Consul dropped his eyes at last. How many bottles since then? In how many glasses, how many bottles had he hidden himself, since then alone?
> —Malcolm Lowry, *Under the Volcano*

This book includes my own recollections about life with an alcoholic parent who frequently consulted Rand(om) McNally before plotting our next move. However, I also weave in stories from juvenile and adult fiction that portray life with a drunken parent. Mary Doll (2000), who encourages her readers to consider fiction a primary tool with which to uncover truth, asks, "Can that which is not fact (fiction, poesis) provide as much insight into facts that stare us in the face?" (p. xvii). Literature is an integral component of a thorough exploration of the Geographic Cure. School personnel, counselors, and education professors could gain much insight by reading stories that provide a wide-open window onto the world of Children of Alcoholics. The books I discuss and others of a similar nature should, in my opinion, be part of teacher preparation requirements, as well as included in classroom collections of novels to be shared. With educators in mind I also draw upon memoirs of contemporary Adult Children of Alcoholics who describe their own erratic childhoods—particularly Jeanette Walls (*The Glass Castle*, 2005) and Michael Keith (*The Next Better Place*, 2004), both of whom, as children, lived life on the run with a drunk parent. These two particular books contribute, with precision and nuance, a painfully accurate description of life as a Geographic Cure Child.

While conducting research for my project, I was reminded of a novel that I read as a teenager, one which startled me with its grim frankness about alcoholism: Émile Zola's *L'Assommoir* (1877/2007). The novel came back to me the minute I read the opening of Walls' 2005 book, *The Glass Castle*, which begins with a passage about Walls riding (as an adult) past a dumpster in which her mother was scrounging for food. When I read that description, Zola's character Gervaise, a 19th-century dumpster diver, flashed back into my mind. Until I was 16 years old, I was not aware of literary connections to my home life. I read *L'Assommoir* in my junior year of high school, when the school counselor, Mr. Brown, enrolled me (the new kid who could read well) into an independent study course for English. The English teacher, Mr. Withers, gave me a list of books to check out from the library, but also handed me a couple of his own copies of novels that were not on the list. *L'Assommoir* was one of those novels; I devoured it whole. I discovered that my mother was much like Gervaise and her husband Coupeau, who reassured themselves about their own drinking by contending that only hypocrites say they never drink. Zola's characters were also certain that wine was harmless, and in fact healthy, and that wine would not make people drunk. At one point in her life my mother, six months out of a 28-day residential rehab program, began drinking wine with that very same justification. In her mind, the fact that she never returned to bourbon meant she was successfully "dry." Nine or ten gallons of Gallo per week didn't count. Today I wonder if Mr. Brown, who had already encountered my mother when she registered me for school, spoke with Mr. Withers before I began that class. Both the counselor and the teacher helped me make sense of my world on several occasions during my time at that school. Mr. Withers required me to write response papers for each book. In responding to Zola's novel, I wrote volumes.

While Zola's Coupeau and Gervaise were destroying themselves physically and emotionally with their alcoholism, their daughter Nana turned to prostitution as a coping mechanism. In my own case, I clung to books. Fiction and poetry were my floating bridges—they helped me get across each raging current. A handful of books (Louisa May Alcott's *Little Women* (1868/1947), first and foremost) were my most sacred treasures, stashed in a box during each move until we landed at the

CHAPTER 1

next arbitrary spot. Once unpacked, those friends stood ready to offer not only a means of escape, but advice on growing-up matters that I found in no other source. For example, I learned right along with Amy in *Little Women* about the perils of selfishness, and from her mother, "Marmee," I discovered how important it is to help people in need. I had few academic achievements, and was totally inept in math, but I excelled in reading from the time I was four. This thrilled a teacher here or there, prompting a few to give me books to keep. Having my "nose in a book" at home often got me in trouble, after about the second or third drink for Marcia. My mother might have been drunk, but she wasn't stupid. She knew that books were my escape routes. Therefore, even though she, when sober, loved to read, it angered her to see me engrossed in someone else's story.

How very fortunate for me that reading allowed me the emotional hiding place I needed. However, it would have been exceedingly helpful for me to have read about other children in my peculiar predicament. I would have benefitted greatly from learning how my fictional contemporaries were dealing with their own parental alcoholism issues. Doll (2000) writes, "My belief is that theory needs the wisdom of writers [who are] the closest our culture can come to wisdom figures" (p. xviii). I completely agree. I could have used more wisdom figures, earlier on.

A contemporary juvenile novel that was not around when I was a middle-school child, but which could be a huge help to young Children of Alcoholics today, is a book titled, *I Almost Love You, Eddie Clegg,* by Audrey Supplee (2004). This novel is a first-person account of life with a drunken parent, written from the viewpoint of Asa, a 13-year-old girl. The book chronicles the backsliding of Asa's stepfather, Eddie, who falls off the wagon (again) after losing his job. In one chapter, Asa is told by her stepdad to retrieve a bottle of vodka that he has hidden the back of *her* closet. The seal is broken; the bottle is not full. Eddie explains to Asa the purpose of asking for the bottle:

"I probably won't drink it anyway. Just wanted to look at it. Kind of a test, ya know? A pop quiz. To prove I can resist it." He looked up again. "See? Willpower."

I waited for a silent count of twenty. "Want me to put it back now?" I asked.

He shook his head. "Leave it." He swivelled back to his computer. (Supplee, 2004, p. 64)

In this novel Asa covers for Eddie and begins telling a string of lies, in order to keep peace in the household, but also in order to manipulate Eddie into telling a few lies for her in return. The themes of secrets, lies, and disappointments run thick and fast through this little book. Children who live through days similar to Asa's would find, in effect, a friend who understands. If teachers read the book, they might understand that secret-keeping and dystopic thinking constitute a crucial skill set—survival mechanisms—for Children of Alcoholics. "Dystopia is critical of the concept of hope," explains Marla Morris (2001, p. ix). Children of Alcoholics feel burned many times over by hope, and Asa is no exception. Supplee's novel provides a dead-on illustration of parental alcoholism, and there are other novels and memoirs that offer true glimpses into the harrowing experience of being a Child of an Alcoholic. This study is fortified with such literary glimpses, in order to provide a space for fiction and memoir to tell the truth.

I make no presumption that the general subject of Children of Alcoholics is anything new. The research on parental alcoholism is vast. Within the fields of medicine, sociology, psychiatry, and psychology alone, there is well over a century of research to be found about this particular addiction and its effect upon the children of those who are addicted. Yet there is not much work that specifically addresses the topic of school-aged Children of Alcoholics whose parents habitually relocate, nor the consideration of how those chronic moves affect the children's experiences at school. Additionally, I have not found *any* research regarding spaces where curriculum theory and the Geographic Cure intersect. And yet, there is much to be explored about that intersection within our field. My hope is that I'm only beginning the conversation about what it means for a child to live in manic scramble mode at home, yet be expected to perform well at school. It is in the field of curriculum theory that *perspective* is recognized as a contributing research tool. Alice Pitt (2003) explains:

> Research that explores in greater depth the lived experiences of groups of people historically marginalized within education in order to affect educational policy, practices, and institutional structures seeks to transform knowledge about such groups by eliciting, directly or indirectly, their perspectives. Here meaning is made from experience. (pp. 4–5)

Therefore, I use a few of my own lived experiences and the real or fictional experiences of other Children of Alcoholics to provide a greater depth of understanding of a child's life ruled by pandemonium and instability at home. Additionally, I assert that pandemonium (read: defensiveness against low school performance as perceived by educational powers-that-be) rules children's lives at school as well. Martha Whitaker (2006) explains:

> Abusive curriculum stands in the way of well-intentioned teachers moving toward the challenging yet invigorating goal of making spaces for living a dream of community and social justice.... Like the emotional abuser described in psychological tomes, a curriculum that is exclusive and technical, grounded in theories of Western rationality, develops from intense insecurity and the need to control. The greater the sense of chaos and threat to the power of the status quo, the more tightly curriculum has been crafted. (p. 42)

Unfortunately, Geographic Cure Children are among the kids most vulnerable to this type of teacher-controlling school "reform." Tight control is what drove Ms. Jones to pry Stevie away from the teacher who could best help him grow.

CHAPTER 1

THE SINGULAR SET OF CHILDREN OF ALCOHOLICS

> Dad is back. I mean, he called. He hasn't been in touch with us in weeks. I really thought he was gone forever. I wish he WERE gone forever. I like it so much better when he's out of our lives.
> —Paula Danziger and Ann M. Martin,
> *Snail Mail No More*

Geographic Cure Children do not exactly fall into our laps pre-identified, and parents most certainly do not bring their alcoholism to the attention of school staff. Since "most 'problem drinkers,' including those with children, do not seek professional help" (Cuijpers, 2005, p. 446), the task of estimating even a general number of Children of Alcoholics is a difficult process. Most current estimates put the number of Children of Alcoholics at 29 million, with *11 million under 18 years old* (Cuijpers, 2005; Grant, 2000; NACOA, n.d.). It takes a caring, intuitive adult to open up possibilities for such children to identify themselves and seek help. Yet if Children of Alcoholics move in and out of schools frequently, the likelihood of the kids seeking help decreases even more.

A highly mobile child's permanent record—or lack of one altogether—tells a story. The U.S. Census Bureau (2011) reports that in just one year, from 2009–2010, 37.5 million people in the U.S. moved from one household location to another. Of those 37.5 million, 69.3% moved within the same county, 16.7% moved to a different county within the same state, and 11.5% moved to a different state. The remaining 2.5% moved abroad. The top two reasons given for moving were "housing" (43.7%) and "family concerns" (30.3%) (U.S. Census Bureau, 2011). There are no statistics from the Census Bureau on how many "family concern" moves were driven by spontaneous decisions of inebriated parents. However, from my own experience and from what I have observed during nearly 30 years in education, I feel that it's safe to say that alcohol could have fueled some of those "family concerns." When moving becomes a pattern, rather than an isolated or occasional instance, the children in those families have a very tough time. The increasing number of transient school-aged children has become the focus of research over the last two decades:

> As the problems and opportunities that accompany moving have become more apparent, attention has broadened from individuals who initiate moves to the spouses and children who accompany them. . . . A crucial way in which these changes are played out over time involves the educational transitions and trajectories of the children of families that move. (Hagan, MacMillan, & Wheaton, 1996, June, p. 369)

Family relocations can be stressful for children even when alcohol is not a factor. Just the "new kid" dynamic alone can overwhelm a child. Winnicott (2004) tells us that "cultural experience begins with creative living first manifested in play" (p. 100), but because play is warped by both the volatility of the drunk parent and the isolation of the child, cultural experience is stilted. Wood, Halfon, Scarlata, Newacheck, and Nessim (1993) describe the traumatic impact that moving has upon children:

> A family move disrupts the routines, relationships, and attachments that define the child's world. Almost everything outside the family that is familiar is lost and changed. Even a short move, which may allow the parents to maintain their network of supports and relationships, may force the child to change schools and friends. Thus, the child has to develop new friendships and adjust to a new curriculum and new teachers. A family move is especially stressful if it is not wanted or if the family has limited resources to deal with the move. (p. 1337)

When the adult making the decision to move also happens to be an alcoholic, the move is indeed quite likely to be "not wanted" and irrational. Additionally, the phrase "limited resources" takes on an even deeper meaning when there is only one parent, and that one parent is not making decisions with the best interests of the child in mind. Time, attention, and love are rare commodities. For children who lack these resources already, sporadic moves are earth shattering. This interweaving of family mobility and parental alcoholism produces the singular set of Children of Alcoholics who are Geographic Cure Children.

Certainly, professionals in the fields of education, school counseling, school nursing, social work, and community action groups are aware that parental alcoholism affects children. However, I am asserting that most of those professionals do not fully understand the fearful, confusing, shaky-ground life of Geographic Cure Children. Perhaps readers of this book who are likely to encounter Geographic Cure Children might discover in themselves a desire to know more about this phenomenon. Educators and others who work with children may not have read the most recent best-selling memoir of an Adult Child of an Alcoholic. They may, in fact, have only a vague notion of what Children of Alcoholics in general go through, and how many of those children's basic needs are not being met. *Understanding* would be even more difficult when, for such children who are also transient students, interactions with adults outside the boundaries of immediate family are sparse and superficial. When interactions with adults occur, the family secret remains intact, guarded at all costs. This is why I hope to add to an understanding of such children in peril. My expectation is that I may find readers who become passionate about helping a Geographic Cure Child imagine his/her own future, beyond the immediate turmoil. Maxine Greene (2001) contends that imagination should be "central in education and scholarship. Imagination is the capacity to posit alternative realities. It makes possible the creation of 'as if' perspectives" (p. 65). Geographic Cure Children need educators who can help them develop such perspectives.

This is why I stand alongside Ted Aoki (2005) against, as he termed it, "a curricular demand for sameness [that] may diminish and extinguish the salience of the lived situation of people in classrooms" (p. 362). The greatest example that I see of this "sameness" stems from school systems' alarm over the requirements of the federal No Child Left Behind Act, which impacts transient children most

CHAPTER 1

of all. While immersed in objectives and standards, with one eye always on the testing calendar, many schools consider the mid-year newcomer as a nuisance, an intruder even, and a test-average-buster. Few care one whit about that new child's lived experiences—especially when the school's "Needs Improvement" alert level is on red. What the policy makers seem to forget, as they push states into the much-maligned newest versions of the Adequate Yearly Progress and Learning Objective feeding frenzy, is that children are not going to learn until they feel the importance of learning intrinsically. Greene (2009) writes:

> I have suggested that the individual, in our case the student, will only be in a position to learn when he is committed to act upon his world. . . . He may be conditioned; he may be trained. He may even have some rote memory of certain elements of the curriculum; but no matter how well devised is that curriculum, no matter how well adapted to the stages of his growth, learning . . . will not occur. (p. 164)

While many education professionals are quite familiar with the difficulties of helping a child find that commitment to his/her own learning, I wonder how many can imagine what it must be like for a child who is uprooted every time he begins to take an interest in his world. For children who are perpetually new to a class, their world is first and foremost about survival and adjustment during their dreaded "first days of school," which repeat like a stuck needle on a vinyl record album. When they do remain in one place for some length of time, such children are often extremely wary of trusting anyone, including themselves. There are Geographic Cure Children whom I either personally know, or whose memoirs I've read, who *did* find within themselves the desire to engage in the learning process. In those cases, as in my own, there was an adult along the way who valued them, and who helped them decide to trust that their world would eventually improve. One enlightened adult, somewhere along the way . . . it sounds pedestrian, but it is the single best thing that can happen to a Geographic Cure Child. Not that anyone needs to try to be a hero for these children. A significant start for these kids would be to simply find a perceptive adult who does not seem clueless, or helpless, in considering how best to interact with them. If Geographic Cure Children can imagine life beyond the passed-out parent, and can see value in taking a risk and investing themselves in their own learning, they can take those commodities with them on the road. In targeting educators, school counselors, school nurses, and community health workers, as well as those who help such professionals prepare for their fields, I hope to increase awareness of how the Geographic Cure impacts school-aged children, as well as the adults with whom they come into contact—many of whom feel ill-equipped to help.

As part of my effort to deepen the understanding of the lived experience of Geographic Cure Children, I have woven "insets" into the beginnings of Chapters 1 through 5 and the end of Chapter 6. These narrative vignettes illustrate the Life Erratic, portraying an aspect of life with a parent who chronically searches, as the title of Michael Keith's book (2004) puts it, for "the next better place." Stevie, whose story began this introductory chapter, is a composite of several children who attended the schools in which I taught. The insets in Chapters 2 through 5 are autobiographical. In Chapter 6, the inset appears at the end, rather than the beginning, bringing Stevie back into view. This last vignette appears at the end for a specific purpose: While I use my own personal accounts to illuminate life on the road with my alcoholic mother, Stevie opens and closes this book as my figurative call to action. His story is *now*, not decades ago. He and countless more children who are living at the mercy of the Geographic Cure need our attention *today*.

OVERVIEW OF CHAPTERS 2 THROUGH 6

Chapter 2, "The Confounded Life of an 80-Proof Home," surveys the history of substance abuse and the tradition of alcohol use/abuse in America, before narrowing the focus to parental alcoholism specifically. While homing in on alcohol, my intention is neither to discount the rest of the substance-abusing world (illegal drug users, prescription drug abusers) nor suggest that alcohol is not a drug. Children are being raised in mercurial conditions by parents who are addicted to all manner of chemicals, and in many respects my own use of the term "Children of Alcoholics" can be considered a shortened phrase for "children of alcoholics and other substance-abusing parents." However, the downhill slide of a heroin or crack addict is often quicker and more noticeable to outsiders than that of the alcoholic. In most cases a person addicted to "hard" drugs cannot remain under the public radar for as long as someone who "drinks too much." There are distinctions in the circumstance of a child whose parent consumes nothing illegal, and whose drug of choice is woven thickly through the fabric of modern society and is available in grocery stores. Thus, Chapter 2 lays bare the ensuing trauma of children who are secretly subjected to what I've termed "fermented parenting," wherein turmoil and unpredictability rule the day.

In Chapter 3, "The Unhinged Lives of Children on the Move," I set aside parental alcoholism temporarily to investigate family mobility and its impact upon school-aged children. The focus here is on the bleaker side of family relocation. Families with single parents or grandparents are more likely to move than families headed by two parents (Wood et al., 1993), and, for those children, the lack of relationships hits especially hard. Then, on top of everything else, *school* comes into play. When a child is brought to a new teacher mid-year, the teacher may either deliver a defeating blow ("Oh great. I'll have to figure out where to put you."), *or* she can be receptive and welcoming to the child for whatever short period of time they share. Chapter 3 considers the point of view of schools, for which the most common "student mobility problems" include difficulty in obtaining student records and *teacher attitudes* about having a new student thrust upon them at random points in a school year (Bainbridge, 2003; Million, 2000; Knight, Vail-Smith, & Barnes, 1992). Therefore Chapter 3 examines not just the manner in which mobility impacts the child's school experience, but also the ways in which mobile children impact schools.

CHAPTER 1

In Chapter 4, "Drinking and Driving (Away)," I tease out the unique and frightening issues facing children who inhabit the "and": They are subjected to both fermented parenting *and* multiple relocations (at the whim of the alcoholic parent). The convergence of these two lines becomes my focal point. This chapter takes a close look at the emotional distress of children who cannot build a sense of identity of their own, yet who must help the alcoholic parents protect theirs. My contention is that these children's trauma stems not just from the clank of empty bottles alone, nor from frequent relocations alone, but from the powerfully destructive merger of the two. Hall and Webster (2007) write, "The child who deals with additional major stressors beyond alcoholism in the home of origin depletes his/her coping resources even further" (p. 426). To bear the brunt of another new neighborhood, new school, and new level of secrecy is to endure "additional stressors" of mammoth proportions. This is why I contend that this subgroup of Geographic Cure Children are a distinctive, yet largely unrecognized group of fragile children who need our time and attention.

Chapter 5, "Hold Still," takes a side trip down a highway on which I never expected to travel. It is in this chapter that I discuss the lived experience of being derailed by a catastrophic event—cancer—while deep in the middle of writing this book. During the time that I was writing about my illness, I came to call Chapter 5 "the cancer chapter," but in reality it is an account of self-discovery that created an entirely different dimension to my examination of the Geographic Cure. It became evident to me, to a much fuller extent than I'd realized BC (before cancer), that my own "learned behavior" of Geographic Cure-Seeking is very much still entrenched in my *adult self*. This realization forced me to take a second look at my commonalities with cure-seekers in education who seem to be changing everything for the sake of change alone.

Chapter 6, "The Geographic Cure Writ Large," emphasizes that supporting the Geographic Cure Child is uniquely problematic; it's difficult to help a child who is flung into a class mid-year and then hauled back out again soon after. My hope is that an increased understanding of the problem among educators may lead to some complicated but necessary conversations about how we relate to such children during the time we have with them. I also assert that just as the Geographic Cure Child is forced to live the Life Erratic at home, where a cure-seeking parent is calling the shots, many teachers are forced to *work* the Life Erratic because cure-seeking "experts" are calling the shots. I discuss the similarity that I've observed between the reactions of Geographic Cure Children—mistrust, cynicism, disgust at the *fake happy voice*—and the reactions of teachers who are pulled along in the chase for educational cures. Like Ms. Jones, who wants Stevie and Miss Lacey to *suck it up and get on with it*, it seems to me that policy makers want educators to do just the same. How frustrating, when—just like Children of Alcoholics—what many teachers need most is to be able to "stay put" for a while.

CHAPTER 2

THE CONFOUNDED LIFE OF AN 80-PROOF HOME

INSET: OFFICER JAKE'S STEEL-TOE SHOE

The summer before my junior year in high school, we moved from Florida to a small city near Atlanta. Once again I was the "new girl," and it was harder than ever to make friends. But by spring I had a few genuine buddies. I loved them for not asking too many questions about my home life, and I adored them for being so accepting when I took my eight-year-old brother Geoff around with me. Occasionally, however, I tried to be a "normal" teenager, and attend a dance or a party without Geoff. During these atypical times when I took off alone, I always had a twinge in my gut. Going out without taking Geoff meant leaving him alone with our mother, Marcia, who was likely to end up sloshed. I was torn . . . loving the rare, just-us-teens-hanging-out experience, but hating the idea of my little brother dealing with our mother without any buffer. When I did go out, it was only if I gauged Marcia to be relatively sober at the onset of the evening (more likely on Fridays, after work). I knew that the TV would be the babysitter, and that Geoff would carry on our established routine, which was to watch shows that Marcia liked, wait for her to slump over in her recliner, and then watch our own favorites, with the sound turned up to offset the snoring. My brother could then put himself to bed, and I would check on him when I returned.

One night after a dance, a date dropped me off in front of our newest "home": an apartment in a short row of a few old townhouses. At my request the boy did not walk me to the door. He just watched long enough to see me putting my key in the lock, then drove away. The doorknob turned easily, but the door opened only a little before the heavy chain stopped it short. Marcia obviously decided at some point during her own date with Jim Beam to chain the door, so that I'd have to wake her up to be let in.

The recliner was positioned directly in my line of sight, and I could see my mother in all her glory: head cocked to one side, lower jaw loose, bottom teeth pushed out, drool making a run for it. As always, a pile of ash had collected on the carpet, directly under her limp hand, while the butt of a burned-out cigarette still dangled between her fingers. At first I was simply aggravated, and called out to her to come unlock the chain. When she didn't respond, I shouted and started ringing the doorbell. My mother didn't budge. When I hammered the doorbell and still got no response, my legs nearly gave way from fear—Geoff wasn't responding either. I stepped back from the door and found rocks to throw at his upstairs window. No response again. I was terrified that Marcia had flown into a rage and somehow murdered my little brother. Panicking, I pounded on the door of our next-door neighbors, whom we had

CHAPTER 2

made a point to avoid from the day we moved in. They barely recognized me, and were confused and suspicious about why I was standing there after midnight, asking to use their phone.

"Hi. I live next door. I can't get in . . ." I began, trying to appear calm but needing to mow them down. "May I use your phone?" I was hoping that if I called home, Geoff would hear the upstairs phone near his bedroom. The husband ducked behind the door to speak to the wife. Frantically I tried to clarify the situation: "I just need to tell my brother to unlock the chain." Reluctantly they allowed me to come inside, staring wild-eyed at me. Only later did I realize that they didn't have to ask if my mother was home. Thin walls had already exposed our secrets.

When Geoff did not pick up the ringing phone, I felt like I would die from fright. I called the operator and asked for the police. My horrified neighbors listened as I told the dispatcher our whole insane story: My mother's drunk / my brother won't wake up / she's downstairs—I can see her / I see the empty bourbon bottle / he's upstairs I guess; I can't see him / he's eight / I left him alone with her / she seemed OK when I left . . .

The dispatcher asked who was with me, and I realized I didn't even know the people into whose home I'd burst so unceremoniously. When we first moved in, the neighbors tried to be friendly, but my mother shunned them. I was expected to do the same. Now, in this moment of desperate need, I had to ask my next-door neighbors their names. We'd lived there eight months.

The policemen who responded to the call tried to force the door open hard enough to break the chain. That didn't work. The back door was locked with a deadbolt, another dead end. They decided to try opening the large sliding window by the door. However, we had a stick in the window to guard against burglars, so once again access was blocked. The window would only open a few inches. We yelled. We leaned on the doorbell repeatedly. We threw more rocks at Geoff's window. I was petrified. Briefly the policemen discussed ramming the door.

However, "Officer Jake" had the aim of a starting quarterback. He took off one of his steel-toe shoes and hurled it, through the barely-open window, at Marcia's recliner. How he missed my mother's face was amazing, although at that moment I wouldn't have cared if he had beheaded her altogether. The shoe cleanly hit the edge of the recliner near her head, and Marcia stirred a bit. We all yelled some more, and my mother finally woke up enough to stagger to the door. When she unhooked the chain and saw two policemen with me, she rose up to her full height and launched into an indignant, slurring tirade about my obvious attempt to humiliate her. But as she spoke, fumes from our gas stove hit the three of us at the same time. Officer Jake and I pushed past my mother to fly upstairs to my brother. The other officer ran to the oven to cut off the gas, finding a pan of cornbread inside which had burned to black charcoal. My brother was groggy, bewildered, and in pain from a fierce headache. My mother, who cussed like a sailor once we all gathered outside, showed no ill effects from the fumes whatsoever . . . just utter disdain for the neighbors who stood at their doorstep, wringing their hands.

THE CONFOUNDED LIFE OF AN 80-PROOF HOME

RETREATS OF SUBSTANCE

The desire for alcohol is quite peculiarly mental in its origin. It is a matter of mental training and growth, and it is cultivated in social soil. Not one drinker in a million began drinking alone.
—Jack London, *John Barleycorn—Alcoholic Memoirs*

"*Never put off till tomorrow what you can drink today*," that's me.
—Charles Jackson, *The Lost Weekend*

Saying you're an alcoholic *and* a drug addict is like saying you're from Los Angeles *and* California.
—Carrie Fischer, *Wishful Drinking*

There are countless ways that we can instantly change our outlook via ingestion of some kind of organic or manufactured ingredient. In the Neolithic period (8500 B.C.E.-4000 B.C.E.) our ancestors had already figured out what could be done with grapes besides eating them; wine has been around as long as community living (UPMAA, 2008). The Sumerians called the opium poppy "the joy plant" and were cheerfully cultivating the drug in 3400 B.C.E. (Booth, 2008, p. 1). Drugs expand our options, whether we want a way *out*—an escape from emotional or physical pain— or a way *in* to the greener pasture of a different reality. They offer a way to "see things from a special angle," as Burroughs explained (1953/2003, p. 128). Some of us want to be healed, mentally, physiologically, or spiritually. Some of us want to be as productive as humanly possible. Some of us just want a buzz, plain and simple. For many, sobriety is a second-choice modus operandi. However, problems arise when a personal choice becomes an addiction.

In the mid-18th century, American abolitionist Anthony Benezet turned his attention to alcohol and published a stark depiction of addiction. I have a photocopy of the original manifesto, titled, "The Mighty Destroyer Displayed, In Some Account of the Dreadful havock made by the mistaken Use as well as Abuse of DISTILLED SPIRITOUS LIQUORS By a Lover of Mankind [*sic*]," in which Benezet (1774) asserted:

> It is no uncommon thing for habitual rum-drinkers, when a fit of sickness comes on, which they conclude will be their last, to desire to have plenty of rum by them; by which means, they continue intoxicated till death: to so astonishing and deplorable a sottish condition have they reduced themselves! (p. 13)

I find it interesting to see these comments juxtaposed alongside French poet Charles Baudelaire's (1851/2002) declaration, nearly 100 years later, that with wine, "The wicked man becomes abominable, just as the good man becomes truly excellent" (p. 15). Yet Thomas DeQuincey (1821/1998), Baudelaire's British counterpart, preferred opium over wine, claiming that wine "robs a man of his self-possession (while) opium greatly invigorates it" (p. 40). Baudelaire's (1851/2002) praise for the high merit of wine was almost worshipful: "Whoever has had a remorse to appease, a memory to evoke, a sorrow to drown, a castle in the air to build, all, in short, have called on you, the mysterious god hidden in the fibres of the vine" (p. 5).

Whether by wine, opium, THC, acid, or hundreds of other options, the practice of chemically altering one's state of mind continues to flourish—either as a pastime, or as a total way of life. Consumers have expressed countless "reasons why." Huxley (1954/2004) described a need for "frequent chemical vacations from intolerable selfhoods and repulsive surroundings" (p. 64). With staunch conviction Huxley states:

> Most men and women lead lives at the worst so painful, at the best so monotonous, poor and limited that the urge to escape, the longing to transcend themselves if only for a few moments, is and has always been one of the principal appetites of the soul. (p. 62)

Instant gratification via the achievement of an altered state has its appeal. And any compliant "Dr. Happy" will help his patients calm down, "rev up," be sharper, blur the lines, sleep, or tolerate life with any alterations desired. Many people the world over consider escape via chemical vacation to be completely justified. Eigen (2005a) explains, "At times it feels good to slip away from sense, to drop the burden of meaning, to feel senseless and free" (p. 265).

What happens if we begin to prefer the chemically altered "slip-away-from-sense" all the time? The retreat then becomes a one-way ticket, with no desire to return home. "You become a narcotics addict because you do not have strong motivations in any other direction. Junk wins by default," explains Burroughs (1953/2003, p. xxxviii). I would extend this description to any abused substance. There is a single-mindedness to being an addict. Elizabeth Wurtzel (2002) explains that addiction just *is*: "I do drugs to do drugs. . . . [T]he circumstances that got me started on my addiction no longer exist. I'm doing what I'm doing because I just can't stop" (p. 104).

When a traumatized person discovers an acting-out path that best helps him or her avoid feelings, that path can lead to the obliteration of the hurtful memory altogether. Phillips (2001a) explains: "We have to forget what it is we are escaping from—which kinds of feeling, of mood and memory, of desire and encounter—and, ideally, we need to forget that escaping is what we are doing" (p. 61). Perhaps with advances in civilization come advances in levels of human despair. Stressors abound to make many of us feel ready to snap at a moment's notice. By the early 20th century, Artaud (1988) was claiming that we have every right to chemically alter ourselves in any manner that works: "So long as we have failed to eliminate any of the causes of human despair, we do not have the right to try to eliminate those means by which man tries to cleanse himself of despair" (p. 99). Sigmund Freud (1940/1969) asked us not to forget to "include the influence of civilization among the determinants of neurosis. It is easy, as we can see, for a barbarian to be healthy; for a civilized man the task is hard" (p. 42).

Certainly, there are many people who abuse drugs and other substances in an effort to mask emotional trauma. McDougall (1985) writes:

> We are all liable to discharge tension in "acting out" ways when events are unusually stressful (eating, drinking, smoking more than usual, etc.). But those who habitually use action as a defense against mental pain (when thought and the recognition of feeling would be more appropriate) run the risk of increasing their psychosomatic vulnerability.... The signal from the psyche is reduced to an action devoid of words. (p. 95)

We have evolved into a people who now even use drugs to cure problems with drugs. For example, we began to use coca to treat morphine addiction and, as Sigmund Freud (1884/2003) described, as a treatment for acute alcoholism: "The irresistible compulsion to drink was either banished or alleviated, and the dyspeptic complaints of the drinkers were relieved" when coca was employed (p. 33). No wonder John Pemberton—whom Sadie Plant (2001) describes as "a doctor addicted to morphine, called a 'drug fiend' by one of his peers"—pronounced Coca Cola a "great blessing" (p. 72). Plant (2001) quotes Pemberton, who touted his drink as a cure-all for "the unfortunate who are addicted to the morphine or opium habit, or the excessive use of alcoholic stimulants," declaring that "thousands proclaim it the most remarkable invigorator that ever sustained a wasting and sinking system" (p. 72). When the beverage first went on sale, coca *was* an ingredient, Plant writes, noting that Coca Cola was advertised as "the perfect lift for 'turbulent, inventive, noisy, neurotic new America'" (p. 71). A modern tonic for a hectic, modern society: a cure for the cure. And if adults cannot keep up the pace, how can their children? What does the reach for a "tonic" tell the child? This *keeping up* in a society of ever-quickening speed spawns an addiction to the better, the faster. Hop across time zones and you can prolong the sunset for hours. Drink shots of Red Bull and you can be the most alert drunk in the bar. Fly off, then, to the next cool (numbing?) better thing.

Whether prompted by trauma, powerlessness, boredom, the desire for remedy, or flat-out curiosity, the quest for chemical resolution, for mental change, is a cure-seeking undertaking. Some will argue that "recreational users" are seeking no cure at all. However, I feel that even when a drug user has no sorrow to drown, nothing to repair or forget, no woes to contend with, the actual desire to get high for the sake of getting high is still a search for a cure of sorts: "I feel *this* way, but I want to feel some *other* way."

However, I certainly agree that many drug and alcohol abusers never embark on a search for a "cure" that will end their dependence, or even just *something better* (unless it's a better high). They have no interest in ending the addiction at all. For example, Weiss (2003) writes that Artaud was not seeking a fresh start when he went to Mexico looking for "one of the last places on earth where the curative peyote dance still existed, a festival which would liberate his body and illuminate his inner landscape" (p. 162). He was simply pursuing his drug of choice. Artaud's trip did not typify the Geographic Cure.

CHAPTER 2

Whatever the original reasons were for indulging, drug users who become addicts find that they prefer that altered mindset all the time. Those reasons fade away, and the fix becomes the focus. Then comes the abuser's conviction that the drug use is "my business." This is problematic when the personal desire for chemically induced change alters the way one interacts with others. It is at that point that it's not "just about me" anymore. Derrida (1990/2003) writes, "it cannot be said that the pleasure of drug use (*la jousissance toxicomanique*) is in itself forbidden. Rather we forbid a pleasure that is at once solitary, desocializing, and yet contagious for the socius" (p. 37). I take issue with Derrida regarding the concept of "solitary" drug use. A substance-consuming spouse, friend, family member, or coworker might manage to remain *solitary* in her chemical endeavors for a time, if she manages to interact with no one. However, when there are life roles to be played, others are indeed affected by the pleasure-seeker's choices. Parent/child relationships are affected. Jobs are affected. Marriages and friendships are affected. For instance, Edgar Allen Poe's (1843/2003) narrator in *The Black Cat* explains that over several years his personality and character changed for the worse, "through the instrumentality of the Fiend Intemperance" (p. 17); he admits he became "more moody, more irritable, more regardless of the feelings of others. I suffered to use impertinent language to my wife. At length, I even offered her personal violence" (p. 17). The man who privately offers his wife personal violence, like Poe's narrator, can be the public hail-fellow-well-met, who is cheered by his buddies for buying the next round. Alcohol abuse often results in job and family problems, and yet . . .

> at the same time, alcohol is woven into the social fabric of our culture, and indeed many people enjoy the social and cultural connection of sharing a drink together. As mentioned, 88% of Americans have used alcohol at some point in their life; and 65% consider themselves to be current drinkers. (Gunzerath, Hewitt, Li, & Warren, 2011, p. 3)

In other words, the culture of the red Solo Cup—that seemingly ubiquitous drinking vessel found at family picnics and keg parties alike—prevails.

Alcohol consumption is a quintessential social endeavor. By the 19th century in America, alcohol played a starring role in the growing of the country. Rorabaugh (1981) notes that "Fashionable people owned ornate liquor cases or elaborate sideboards that contained numerous bottles of various cordials, including mild, sweet, fruit-flavored elixirs for the ladies," adding that much of the liquor "came from the general store, where its sale was often the most important item of business" (pp. 16–17). This is not to say that every person who drank back then was an alcoholic, any more than is the case today. Rather, my intention is to show the omnipresence of alcohol's function as social bonding instrument through multiple generations. Rorabaugh (1981) makes this plain:

> Alcohol was pervasive in American society; it crossed regional, sexual, racial, and class lines. Americans drank at home and abroad, alone and together, at

work and at play, in fun and in earnest. They drank from the crack of dawn to the crack of dawn. . . . They drank while working in the fields and while travelling across half a continent. They drank in their youth, and, if they lived long enough, in their old age. (p. 21)

My point is that the long history of alcohol's social acceptance complicates the issues surrounding drinking when alcoholism *is* the case. It is easy for an excessive drinker to hide behind the lace curtains of social norms. The alcoholic's drug of choice is ready for purchase at any package shop, grocery, restaurant, or corner convenience store. The user does not get charged with a crime for "possession" unless he is underage. An alcoholic parent tells the children he is doing nothing wrong—he just drinks a bit.

Young children watching happy people advertise alcohol on television believe the alcoholic parent's claim to be *just* a social drinker. (Other adults—new neighbors, colleagues—are also likely to buy that story if their interaction with the drinker is limited.) Children don't understand the disease element of alcoholism. They only see that the desire to escape trumps all. A young Child of an Alcoholic certainly cannot comprehend the fact that the parent might be suffering from his own childhood issues. Perhaps the mom or dad is consumed with melancholy. A melancholic person, explains Jutta Schamp (2002), refuses to let go of the past; she is unwilling to recognize and cope with the pain of loss, and is therefore "locked in a state of permanent depression, ambivalence, self-inhibition or low self-esteem" (p. 86). Schamp's description certainly fits the alcoholic I grew up with. In my teenage years I thought my mother was mourning her two failed marriages to my father, because she often pined away for him when she was drunk. However, true mourning gives in to pain and sorrow, and then gets past them:

To heal the pain, one—according to Freud—has to go through a phase of mourning labor, where people retreat and work through their loss. To deal with this loss, one has to declare the object dead; that is, withdraw one's libido completely from the object. Only such a work of grief, finally, leads to the emotional acceptance of loss, and then people are free and open to life again. (Schamp, 2002, p. 87)

More likely it was melancholia, not mourning, that consumed my mother. Locked in that permanent depressive state, she found it easier to drown her sorrows than recognize the pain of loss. However, over a span of several decades she fooled scores of people who knew her only as a social-drinking coworker or as a neighbor who preferred to keep to herself. (There was one exception to the neighbor rule: If a neighbor also loved to be "in his cups" as much as she did, they became fast friends. Misery, in that instance, *adored* company.)

ABC Liquor stores were more familiar to me than grocery stores. I sat in the car in front of those "package shops" countless times while my mother ran in to "grab a couple of things." Marcia made feeble attempts to keep her bottles hidden *out of*

CHAPTER 2

reach of the children, supposedly, but *out of sight* is the more accurate term. By the time I was eight years old I was astute enough to watch the levels inside the bottles as they lowered, and my mother didn't want me keeping track of her intake. Therefore, she began stashing bourbon in odd places, leaving one bottle out in the open on a high shelf, posing as the only one. In Charles Jackson's novel, *Lost Weekend* (1963), the central character, Don Birnam, found especially creative ways to hide his liquor. Tying string to bottles, Don would hang them outside of the window, and other bottles would end up in the commode:

> He lifted the heavy enameled lid of the water-tank and put it on the toilet-seat. He took one of the bottles by the neck and carefully set it down inside, in the water, fingering around till he was sure it was out of the way of the plunger. He slowly lowered the second bottle in on the other side, and with his hand he pushed the ball up and down till it rode free. (p. 275)

My mother may not have hidden anything in the commode (that I know of), but she found many other places to stash her means of *relaxing with a cocktail* at home, even after spending a few hours at "Happy Hour" after work. My mother frequented Happy Hour because she could not, for the life of her, put on a Happy Face unless she went there first. When I was young and my brother was a toddler, I wondered if any of the people with whom Marcia worked or socialized would quiz each other about why she was still at the bar at 8:00 p.m. when the two of us were waiting at home. They most likely assumed she had a babysitter. Euphemisms such as "after-work get-together" and "unwinding" were meant to soften the fact Marcia was simply out getting drunk, which was phrased as "a little tipsy" if she caught herself staggering in front of us. Interestingly, "the English language includes more synonyms for 'drunk' than for any other word" (Dickson, 2009, p. 7). There is an art to avoid calling a spade, a spade. The reality is that society is conflicted about alcohol:

> At the centre of that inchoate, swirling mass of contradiction, there is, however, a very simple, two-part truth. Alcohol is in its being and essence an ambiguous molecule, an instrument of pleasure and at the same time of pain. And society's response to that molecule is, in all dealings, and with total congruence, itself ambiguous. A congruence of ambiguities: that's the centre of the thing. (G. Edwards, 2003, p. 191)

Perhaps society has mixed feelings about alcohol because in addition to recognizing the potential for abuse, we also, frankly, have an appreciation for the ways in which it affects (heightens, dulls, numbs) our senses. However, these mixed feelings are costly. Lender and Martin (1987) stress that ambivalence is the largest barrier to solving many alcohol-related problems, citing studies that suggest that "more uniform popular views on acceptable drinking behavior would alone (without legal compulsion) reduce alcoholism and related complications" (p. 201). The likelihood of Americans forming a uniform view of *acceptable* drinking behavior would seem to me to be nearly zero; I can more easily see ambivalence thriving instead. The authors are brutally frank in their conclusion that since Americans have "accepted alcohol as a normal part of life," we have also determined that "dealing with the problems of alcohol . . . is an equally normal social function" (Lender & Martin, 1987, p. 204). It seems to me that we are not dealing with the problems well enough, especially in regard to the ramifications of an alcohol-saturated, arbitrary, neglectful upbringing of the Child of an Alcoholic.

Before delving further into the erratic lives of Children of Alcoholics, I feel compelled to pause here and include a word about sympathy. The purpose of this book is *not* to add another "rotten childhood" diatribe to the world's pile of Books Slamming Mother. I use my stories as illustrations for readers who may not have experienced or considered what it feels like to grow up in a fermented home. My intent is to lend credence to this study via an autobiographical slant, because I have "been there." However, this work is not simply a retrospective. Chaos and trauma frame the lives of millions of children living with alcoholic parents *today, now.* Children who live this chaotic life warrant discussion and consideration within the curriculum studies arena. For the purposes of this book, consideration and sympathy are not the same. Jim Garrison (1997) warns about sympathy:

> Sometimes sympathy is condescension or domination cloaked as an offer to help. Conversely, many expect teachers to be self-sacrificing and to ignore their own needs, desires, and dreams. Self-transcending, expansive growth through sympathy, care, and community allow us to stay safely in the center. (p. xvi)

It is in that center space of growth that I wish more educators, and especially education policy makers, would dwell. Deeper insight into the lives of Children of Alcoholics would seem to me to be essential, since there are so many who are attending schools now. This book is my contribution to the beginning step called for by Pinar (2004): "The first step we can take toward changing reality—waking up from the nightmare that is the present state of public miseducation—is acknowledging that we are indeed living in a nightmare" (p. 5). When, in the name of high-stakes testing and accountability, educational policy makers cut off all opportunities for teachers to rely on their intuition and inclination to care, the nightmare of chaos experienced by children in an 80-proof home follows them to school. Their "home problems" cannot be checked at the door, no matter how much their teachers insist otherwise.

FERMENTED PARENTING

> Having your ten-year-old son with you at the office should not be a cue to drink, but it is for me. For all the times we stopped by the Billy Goat on the way to the train and he sat at a table and enjoyed his kiddie cocktail while I conferred with Phyllis at the bar and slurped Jack.
> —Neil Steinberg, *Drunkard: A Hard-Drinking Life*

CHAPTER 2

Later in this study I home in on literal Geographic Cure Children, whose upbringing combines the groundless alcoholic parenting with frequent family relocations. However, in this chapter I lay bare the figurative side of the Life Erratic, which affects nearly all children whose parents abuse alcohol, whether they move around or not. When parents persistently practice fermented parenting, confusion and instability rule. Fluctuation is the order of the day. (These components are further amplified in the home of a single parent who is an alcoholic, where there is no second adult to provide at least some semblance of order.) Children of Alcoholics learn that the only thing they can count on is that "adults will eventually change the rules" (Thompson, 1998, p. 35). Everything shifts with the tide in homes where alcoholism prevails. As Ballard and Cummings (1990) attest, alcoholic homes are characterized by "unpredictability and inconsistency in routines, parenting, and discipline" (p. 195), all of which occur at the precise time when consistency and predictability are needed most for child development.

In Maryann Carver's (2006) memoir about life with her husband, fiction writer Raymond Carver, she recalls their daughter Chris's frank words about her father's alcoholism: "Mr. Whiskey can't help being mean. He can't help insulting everybody, never letting up until he has me or Vance in tears and total confusion. He's no better to you" (p. 297). Chris Carver articulated to her mother what many Children of Alcoholics know: Emotional abuse and bewilderment are par for the course in an alcoholic's home.

Coping with a chronically drunk parent is a treacherous process. Black (1979) explains what it is that Children of Alcoholics have "learned" in order to be able to cope:

> Many of these children learned it was not all right to experience certain feelings like anger or sadness. It did not help to feel. When they showed their sadness, no one was there to comfort them. When they became angry, they found themselves punished. Or when they wanted to talk about anything important, they simply found themselves ignored. It did not take long for these children to learn first, not to express their feelings, and second, not to feel. (p. 25)

This observation of Black's haunts me on two levels. I remember well how important it became not to feel. I worry when I hear teachers complain about children who "just don't care about anything." Much can be happening at home that makes a child steel his emotions against any semblance of feeling. It concerns me that some teachers perceive a child's emotional deadening as simply a case of child-as-thorn-in-my-side. Despite the fact that there are decades' worth of evidence to the contrary, some educators and those who prepare them for teaching still work from the assumption that most students' home lives are the same: stable, "normal," and nurturing. The reality is that typical child development stages become warped when the primary parent is drunk most of the time. Grostein (1999) describes the "heroic tasks" of the infant/toddler, who must "learn to surmount the anxieties of separation, strange situations, and prey-predator relationships," and highlights the importance of the "exploration of play (taking risks)," writing, "Either courage or cowardice (shame, xenophobia, self-consciousness) is fated to develop at this time" (p. 207). When the parent is an alcoholic, healthy development of a child is a gamble. Worst of all is that Children of Alcoholics often endure that which Garbarino (2000) calls "insults to the soul":

> Nothing seems to threaten the human spirit more than rejection, brutalization, and lack of love. Nothing—not physical deformity, not debilitating illness, not financial ruin, not academic failure—can equal insults to the soul. Nothing compares with the trauma of this profound assault on the psyche. (p. 132)

The parent-child relationship is warped in an 80-proof home. In more stable families, the process of participating in rituals and routines is how children learn "the rules, roles, and values of their family and the culture to which they belong" (Haugland, 2005, p. 226). However, when there is parental alcoholism, rules relate to keeping secrets, roles pertain to coping strategies, and values revolve around keeping the raving beast at bay. "Substance abuse can lead to impaired parent-child relationships characterized by low levels of warmth, involvement and attachment, as well as inconsistent discipline," Gance-Cleveland (2004) explains, adding that such family situations are "more prone to disruption and chaos, increasing children's risk for physical, emotional, social and academic problems" (p. 16). And yet some educators and university professors still work under the assumption that children come to school prepared to make *academic success* their biggest priority. I beg to differ. I think that's the exception, not the rule.

Emotional problems, anxiety, and stress factors for Children of Alcoholics are colossal and well documented (Easley & Epstein, 1991; Gance-Cleveland, Mays, & Steffen, 2008; Gruber & Taylor, 2006; Hall & Webster, 2007; Haugland, 2005; Killeen, 1988; Murray, 1998; O'Rourke, 1990; Sale, 2002; Department of Health and Human Services Substance Abuse and Mental Health Services Administration (U.S. Dept. of HHS, SAMHSA), 2007; Windle, 1990, 1996). Researchers Peleg-Oren and Teichman (2006), who reported on multiple studies that examined the causes of social isolation of Children of Alcoholics, found the key causes to be "shame and secrecy" (p. 56). The issues surrounding secret-keeping are tremendous, and many of the emotional stressors in the life of a Child of an Alcoholic are tied to that one family requirement alone. (I address secrecy in more depth later in this chapter.)

Another common problem that Children of Alcoholics experience is a pervasive feeling of guilt if they perceive that they are displeasing others (Crespi & Sabatelli, 1997). Children of Alcoholics very often blame themselves for their parent's drinking and their family's dysfunctional characteristics. Many of these kids believe that if they were *better* or *smarter*, the parent's alcohol abuse would stop. This leads to feelings of guilt and shame because they aren't able to make everything work out for their family. These children have very likely experienced feelings of worthlessness (Lambie & Sias, 2005). Parents are supposed to help children come into their own as viable human beings. But, as Forward and Buck (1989) explain, "Many of these children, deprived of adequate time, attention and care, begin to feel invisible—as if they don't exist" (p. 41). They may eventually become engulfed in the feeling of being "nothing," and may use that emotion defensively, in the same manner as Winnicott's (1989a) young patient Mark, who, in session, drew his first initial, "M," and explained, "It's a nothing" (p. 376). Winnicott explains that Mark "reached an extreme defense, for if he is a nothing then he cannot be killed or hurt by the worst trauma imaginable" (p. 376). As alarming as it is to think that any child would believe he or she has no value, the truth of the matter is that self-esteem is a foreign concept to many Children of Alcoholics.

Like parents, educators are also supposed to help children come into their own. However, it's a wonder that any educator can do so when children come to school bearing so many emotional wounds. In many cases, the weight of the damage heaped upon these children is more than many adults could bear. There are instances when the teacher in the classroom has no idea what is going on at home, and instances when the teacher doesn't want to know. Yet children, and especially adolescents, hope that a caring adult will figure out the score. In their study of disclosure among adolescent Children of Alcoholics, Tinnfalt, Erksson, and Brunnberg (2011) found:

> Some of the adolescents described taking very concrete steps to verbalize their situation, for example choosing to write an essay at school. They could also choose to read a book about COA. In these cases the child or adolescent expected the teacher to understand something was wrong, and that he or she should acknowledge this. The adolescents also described writing a letter, writing in their diary, or communicating on the internet. The verbalization of the problem was a way for them to raise their level of consciousness, and practice narrating the story. They could start communicating with strangers or imaginary people, which Lena [one girl in a focus group] described as being "just to get it all out of me somehow." (p. 139)

This is why I see the need to bring the concept of "fermented parenting" into curricular thought. Complicated conversations are uncomfortable; they leave heavy implications in the air that disturb our thoughts long after the talking stops. However, this book is meant to begin the dialogue about Geographic Cure Children, and encourage educators to, as Morris (2006) phrases it, "'make room' for them in the curriculum" (p. 132).

Individual Children of Alcoholics tend to craft for themselves a survival mode that is universal to the group at large. In her landmark research on Children of Alcoholics, Black (1979) identified three regularly recurring roles that seem to allow Children of Alcoholics to survive in alcoholic homes. Black explained that the roles are "compensatory changes or reactions to parental alcoholism," which allow the children to survive and maintain stability (p. 24). The three roles identified are: "The Responsible One"—usually the eldest child, who takes care of herself, siblings, and the parent, providing "structure and stability . . . in an often inconsistent setting" and who learns to make daily goals; "The Adjuster"—who does not feel the burdens of the elder child, but follows directions and learns to adjust to whatever is on tap for the day; and "The Placater"—who is sociable and who "greatly needs to smooth over conflicts" (Black, p. 24). I was certainly The Responsible One, and it seems to me that my little brother assumed both The Adjuster and The Placater roles over time. Primarily, though he functioned as The Placater, trying to keep both his mother and sister in a good mood.

Sticking to one's role in the family is "an effort to introduce predictability and peace into the system" (Veronie & Fruehstorfer, 2001, p. 56), which Children of Alcoholics feel is their highest priority. As The Placater, Geoff took charge of our mother's disposition, much as children of depressed mothers do; Winnicott (1989a) writes that such children feel obligated to entertain their mothers in order "to deal with the mother's depressed mood" (p. 247). Winnicott explains that children of depressed mothers are always trying to get to the point where the mother is *not* depressed, but by the time they do, "they are exhausted and need to rest so that they cannot get on with their own lives" (p. 248). In explaining Green's concept of "the dead mother," Sekoff (2005) describes children who are "attempting to enliven a depressed, bereft, or absent mother" (p. 113). This is exactly what Children of Alcoholics do, and it is a tremendous burden, this job of pulling the mother from the edge of a black hole, day after day.

Before Geoff was born, I dealt with that undertaking single-handedly. I was executing the duties of what McDougall (1985) calls "the cork child"—the one "needed to keep the mother together" (p. 119). What an especially perfect term for the Child of an Alcoholic! Geoff was much better at keeping the beast at bay than I was, but we both pulled that duty for many years. Children of Alcoholics seem to feel intrinsically charged with the task of keeping the alcoholic parent on an even keel. Often children think that if their parents are happy enough, they won't drink, which is an even stronger reason to try to alleviate the gloom. Geoff kept our mother busy while I heated TV dinners and poured bourbon down the sink. Feeling that weight of being The Responsible One, I felt that if I tried hard enough, I could find a way to *cure* her. In my ignorance I thought that "out of sight, out of mind" would apply to the heavy glass bottles stashed in those predictable hiding places. I felt it was my duty to bring sobriety into the home. Naturally, I failed.

The older Child of an Alcoholic wants to shield younger siblings from trauma whenever possible, and teach them the fine arts of reading moods, staying out of the way, and deflecting arguments. Many family fights cannot be deflected, though, and Children of Alcoholics end up listening to (or being part of) shrieking and sobbing, night after night. If a situation at school results in the Child of an Alcoholic being treated angrily by an adult other than the alcoholic parent, or even just being talked to in a stern manner, he or she often falls apart. Children of Alcoholics don't "do" conflict. They display unique responses to adult anger, as Ballard and Cummings (1990) report: "Children of Alcoholics can be expected to display more intense emotional responses to anger, because children with increased exposure to anger respond more intensely to it; that is, they become sensitized" (p. 195). In regard to their own feelings, however, Children of Alcoholics have a tendency to suppress anger (Hart & McAleer, 1997). In my experience, suppressing anger was necessary if we hoped to avoid the shouting matches, fear, and sleep deprivation, all of which made for a difficult day ahead in school.

Children of Alcoholics bring to school the learned behaviors that they have acquired from their parents, chief among them being inconsistency in the way they handle stress. Powell and Garcia (1991) assert:

> When Children of Alcoholics leave home they bring to the school environment a myriad of behaviors that have developed from living with an alcoholic. In general, Children of Alcoholics exhibit what can be labeled as bipolar behavior. Some . . . attempt to compensate for their low self-esteem and poor self-image by becoming compliant overachievers; others, though fully capable of performing above average in the classroom, underachieve. (p. 1)

As a very young elementary student, I vacillated between being a smiling little teacher-pleaser who was crushed if ever a harsh word came my way, to being a recluse who spoke little and kept my head down. If the child is an only child, or the last remaining child at home, the absence of a buffer makes life a particular hell all its own. At least siblings or other non-drinking family members can commiserate with, distract, and care for each other. The older ones end up with little time to dwell on how neglected they are; they are too busy being primary care providers. Younger Children of Alcoholics with siblings are shielded somewhat from the most outright manifestations of neglect. The solitary Child of an Alcoholic, however, is *alone* in the most egregious of senses. All Children of Alcoholics, regardless of birth order, are overlooked by the parent who is chronically drunk. When there is no overt sign of parental negligence (no unwashed hair or dirty clothes to draw the eye), emotionally neglected children often dwell under the radar. And even if a host of resulting problems manifest themselves in the child's demeanor or academic performance, neglect is not considered a factor when the family ruse has worked efficiently. Asserting that neglect is "the absence of caring," Sexias and Youcha (1985) note, "People who have been treated like 'nothings' never see themselves as competent or able to cope on their own with ordinary, day-to-day living. But this is hard to recognize as neglect" (p. 23). Older children want to rebel against fermented parenting, but the cost is sometimes too high to sustain the desire. Mary Doll (2002) describes a "highly charged" relational dynamic as one of "strong oppositional feelings [that] can be seen as a kind of emotional energy field" (p. 199). As the Child of an Alcoholic grows up, this energy field can become internalized, making the child ill, or resulting in violence between the parent and child or between the child and others, if "acting out" occurs.

In my case, the nerve to confront Marcia about her drinking increased each year, and by the time I was a teenager we fought about it continually. Our dynamic was similar to the fictional parent/child dynamic created by Canadian writer Dennis Foon, whose play *Liars* (1993) portrays the lives of two teens, Lenny and Jace, both of whom who have alcoholic parents. The staging notes for this play call for the use of life-sized dummies of Jace's dad and Lenny's mom, symbolizing the adults' alcoholism. The faces, shapes, and clothing of the dummies are meant to resemble the parents. In every scene involving the parents, the dummies are always present, used as "protectors and playmates for the parents," and also, in the case of Jace's father, as "a weapon, with which to smash Jace to the ground" (Foon, 1993, p. 57). The play is a realistic rendering of what life is like for teenage Children of Alcoholics. Here, Foon (p. 105) has Lenny challenge his mother:

LENNY: [. . .] I'm worried sick about you. I keep thinking that I'm helping you, but it never stops, you're just getting worse.
MOTHER: You are exaggerating. I don't have a problem. Most adults drink. It is a socially acceptable way to entertain, to relax.
LENNY: All the time?
MOTHER: In moderation.
LENNY: You don't drink in moderation, you're drunk all the time.

When fights with my mother escalated, neighbors could hear every word. Yet I was naïve enough, even in my later teen years, to think we were keeping the family secret intact. We did not have long-term neighbors the way some kids did; there was no one on the block we could claim as an "adopted" family. Most did not try to get to know us after the first few brush-offs from Marcia. Therefore, with one exception, there was no neighbor to whom I could unburden myself. A few times when we moved, it was to "go be near" an aunt, cousin, or old friend of Marcia's. On those occasions I hoped that the relatives or friends would be able to intervene and take charge. Some did try, especially my grandmother, who at various points attempted to live with us. However, Marcia would always decide that being near relatives or friends was a mistake after all. They ended up walking on eggshells around her as much as we did, and she froze them out with her haughtiness and denials. The last time my grandmother tried to live with us, my mother pushed her over the edge. When Marcia was particularly venomous one evening, and my grandmother yelled, "You go to the devil!" and slammed a door in my mother's face. My jaw dropped to the floor. That was the closest my grandmother had ever come to cursing. Alcoholic relatives have that effect on people.

TAKING OVER

Parents who are chronic drinkers often cannot nurture healthy relationships with their children. They may wish they could. Mine would wake me in the middle of the night and slobber in my ear, begging for approval or forgiveness, fishing for forced "of-course-I-love-you" reassurances. However, those encounters are nowhere near the parent/child "mutuality" that Buber (2004) describes:

Because this human being exists: therefore he must be really there, really facing the child, not merely there in spirit. . . . He need possess none of the perfections which the child may dream he possesses; but he must really be there.... If he has really gathered the child into his life then that subterranean dialogic, that steady potential presence of the one to the other is established and endures. Then there is reality between them, there is mutuality. (pp. 116–117)

The only "steady potential presence" in the alcoholic's home is the specter of the next drink that hovers overhead. The only real mutualities between the alcoholic parent and the child are the secrets kept between them and the understanding that the child must step into parenting shoes, regardless of how young she is.

Alcohol-dependent parents need their children to provide "physical care and emotional support, which includes listening, comforting and approving. They become, in effect, the parents of their parents; their efforts shield the family's disorganization from prying eyes" (Seixas & Youcha, 1985, p. 16). "Parentification" happens most often when the alcoholic is a single parent, but it also occurs even when there is a second parent in the picture. The alcoholism of the one, and the enabling by the other, commonly foster this need for the child to take over. Burnett, Jones, Bliwise, and Ross (2006) found "empirical validation for the concept of unpredictability in the family system" to be a primary factor in allowing parentification to develop (p. 186). Parenting the parent is a way for children to cope with the inconsistencies they encounter daily. They learn the fine art of taking control, in order to "bring some sense of control to an otherwise uncontrollable situation" (Burnett et al., 2006, p. 186). Children of Alcoholics need to feel that they can control *something* with the same urgency with which they need oxygen. (The need to be in charge manifests itself in ugly ways by the time they become *Adult* Children of Alcoholics, but "control" is a topic for another book, another time.)

Taking over for the parent and functioning without the parent are situations familiar to almost any Child of an Alcoholic. The first part of the novel by Catherine Ryan Hyde, *The Year of My Miraculous Reappearance* (2007), artfully demonstrates parentification. The author writes from the perspective of a 13-year-old girl named Cynnie, who, for quite some time, has been taking care of her drunk mother and her baby brother, Bill, who has Down's syndrome. The alcoholic parent is completely dependent upon the child to clean up after all of her messes: physical, emotional, and societal. Cynnie is ultra-responsible and is up for the task each day, for her brother's sake. In my own experience as the older sister, I did not resent taking care of my little brother either. The protective factor kicks in when the sibling is born.

For the youngest Children of Alcoholics in the family, there is an added layer of turmoil. Younger ones are expected to listen to the drunk parent, the pseudo-parent sibling, and all manner of others who enter and leave, imposing their own canons. Sometimes there are dozens of chiefs. Other times there are none. When the older children leave home, younger ones are tossed into the center of the storm, with no one left to deflect the thunder. The young ones step up to take their turn as The Responsible Ones, battening down the hatches of the 80-proof home before the next tempest hits.

Parentification is illustrated perfectly in the "Joey Pigza" series, by juvenile fiction author Jack Gantos, about young Joey, whose father is an alcoholic. As a fifth-grade teacher years ago, I loved reading the Joey Pigza books with my students. They enjoyed (and identified with) Joey's mishaps at school and home, but what I loved was that the book opened up spaces for class discussions about parents who drink too much. Via our reader response journals, I would learn that a child here or there was having similar problems with a parent. Sometimes that child and I were able to have meaningful conversations with each other in private. (This is why I wish there were more juvenile fiction stories about Children of Alcoholics.) In *Joey Pigza Loses Control*, Joey is dismayed to learn that his father has fallen off the wagon once again:

> Dad put the bottle to his lips and tilted the bottom up for a moment and when he set it down it was empty. In an instant he had his hand wrapped around another. "That first one was so lonely, it needs a friend to keep it company," he said, smiling.
>
> "Dad," I started, but before I could say anything else he read my mind and started talking.
>
> "It's beer," he replied, and held it up for me to see. "Drinking beer is not like drinking whiskey or vodka. It's beer. You know, soda pop for grownups." (Gantos, 2000, pp. 87–88)

Interestingly, in this book Joey has to wear a patch that delivers medicine to treat his Attention Deficit Disorder. He is being forced by his mother, under pressure from his school, to "control himself," while his father is incapable of doing the same.

ON REFUSING TO TALK ABOUT IT

> It takes a tremendous amount of energy to keep the charade going. The child must always be on guard. He lives in constant fear that he may accidentally expose and betray the family. To avoid that, he often avoids making friends and thereby becomes isolated and lonely.
> —Susan Forward and Craig Buck, *Toxic Parents: Overcoming their Hurtful Legacy and Reclaiming Your Life*

> "I want to know the truth," Sidda said.
>
> "We don't deal in truth," Caro said. "But I've got some stories. Will that do?"
> —Rebecca Wells, *Divine Secrets of the Ya-Ya Sisterhood*

The need for secret-keeping in alcoholic families is critical (Adger, MacDonald, & Wenger, 1999; Ballard & Cummings, 1990; Forward & Buck, 1989; Robinson & Rhoden, 1998). This is a primary reason why so many unidentified Children of Alcoholics remain undetected as they move through schools, churches, and neighborhoods. Lambie and Sias (2005) describe how the keeping of secrets can take on extraordinary force:

> An example of a common family rule and norm of an alcohol-abusing family is the "family secret." The family secret is established so members of the family will not openly discuss the family's dysfunctionality (e.g., alcohol abuse, child abuse, and spousal abuse). In time, maintaining the secret may become a dominating force within the family. (p. 3)

To be the child of a parent who drinks does not necessarily mean being subjected to fermented parenting. However, if the parent needs a drink so badly that he or she will find alcohol any way possible, there's likely to be neglect at hand. Imagine being the child of these two parents, portrayed in J. P. Miller's *The Days of Wine and Roses* (1973), who are this desperate to drink:

> JOE: (*Disgusted.*) Vanilla extract.
> KIRSTEN: (*Practical.*) Thirty-five percent alcohol. (*Joe opens bottle, offers it.*) You need it worse than I do. (*Joe drinks.*) How is it? (*She watches him enviously.*)
> JOE: Not bad. (*Drinks again.*)
> KIRSTEN: Could I—? (*He gives her bottle. She drinks.*) Too sweet. It'll make me sick.
> JOE: Shall I kill it? (*She hesitates, reluctant to let it go.*)
> KIRSTEN: Well—maybe it won't . . . (*She drinks again, hands bottle to Joe. He finishes it, drops it in garbage bag.*) (p. 75)

Not quite resorting to vanilla extract, my mother would nevertheless buy the very cheapest booze possible—brands that she and her friends would jokingly call "rotgut."

In addition to all of the problems that abound behind locked doors in alcoholic homes, the trauma doesn't end when the doors open. As Gruber and Taylor (2006) point out, there is "social humiliation and shame a child may experience as the result of public exposure of their parent's substance abuse or its effects" (p. 13). Fear of public exposure is huge for the child and the parent. Any Child of an Alcoholic who has had a drunk parent show up at school, or at some function, knows this shame. There is also fear of stigma, which is why so many kids clamp shut about parental alcoholism. Arman (2000) points out that despite the fact that the number of Children of Alcoholics in the U.S. is "staggering," studies show that "only a small fraction of these children receive assistance. . . . The denial, secrecy, and isolation present in alcoholic families often keeps children from being identified and helped" (p. 290). If my mother had even a hint that I talked about her drinking to a friend's parent, a teacher, or, heaven forbid, a neighbor, I would have been in a world of trouble. Marcia was convinced that she most certainly was not an alcoholic, and if I suggested otherwise she accused me of melodrama and overreacting. Additionally, she did not want me talking about her ever, period, because she did not want to invite neighborly visits or questions from school. It was understood that I was to maintain the family charade at all costs, a requirement quite typical in alcoholic families:

> Because parental alcoholism is a secret both within and outside the family, children are made partners in the family's denial that a parent is drinking. Children of Alcoholics survive by hiding their parents' problems, pretending everything is normal, and trying to avoid being discovered. (Robinson & Roden, 1998, p. 35)

I learned early on that lying outright, or at the very least withholding information, was what I was expected to do in order to remain in my mother's favor. Lambie and Sias (2005) explain that "family members, including children, will make unhealthy modifications to preserve family equilibrium in the presence of alcohol abuse" (p. 3). I made unhealthy modifications from the time I could talk, as did my brother later on, and we maintained our secrets for years. My curriculum studies colleague, Debbie Burnette, noticed that for this book, I use a pseudonym for my mother, even though she died over a decade ago. I thought that my doing so was simply a matter of not speaking ill of the dead, but my wise friend suggested that perhaps I am still the keeper of secrets, covering for my mother, even today.

Evidently secret-keeping in our family was a multi-generational trait. My mother kept her father's drinking undisclosed as well. Family secrets aren't unusual; there were secrets even in the Freud household. "Usually when things are kept secret, individually or within a family . . . it's because something is wrong, something has gone awry . . . and it's best not to tell anyone about it," Menaker (2001) writes, in regard to Anna Freud's analysis by her own father (p. 89). Anna remained devoted to Freud despite the uncomfortable position she must have been in as a child on his couch. My mother remained devoted to her hard-drinking father, despite the fact that he never sided with her publicly in any of her battles with her mother. Their bond was their secret; he taught her how to hold her liquor when she was in her teens. My grandmother's depression and disappointment with her life were also closely guarded secrets, and were considered the "understandable reasons" why my grandfather drank. The father-daughter tie was strong. When my grandfather died, my mother cried inconsolably for weeks. She carried on their bond every time she uncapped a bottle. And in the grand tradition of my mother's own childhood, the rules in our house were like those of my grandparents: Be suspicious of questions; and don't be upset about anything that goes on. We were a "closed system," as J. T. Edwards (1998) describes:

> In order to support secret keeping, families with alcohol abuse problems tend to be closed systems with rigid boundaries. . . . Their norms and roles become ingrained, not allowing other systems such as schools, other families, and health care agencies to intervene or influence the family system. (p. 3)

My father lived several states away and only saw me during summer breaks from school and a few holiday breaks. Dad knew that Marcia was still drinking, and often tried to get specifics from me, in order to ascertain whether or not he needed to call social services to check on us. I lied to Dad and said it was never "that bad." Lambie and Sias (2005) explain: "The family secret is established so members of the family will not openly discuss the family's dysfunctionality (e.g., alcohol abuse, child abuse, and spousal abuse)" (p. 3).

As chief guardians of secrets, Children of Alcoholics are not always recognized in schools. They learn early on in their young lives that no one talks about the parent's drinking, and that there is hell to pay if boundaries are crossed. Worse than being "in trouble" for talking are the ramifications of the extra rounds that will be consumed by the parent in order to alleviate the stress of being "falsely accused." This urgent need to keep quiet is confusing to young Children of Alcoholics, especially if they visit other households and come to realize that not all children are raised in such a manner. Murray (1998) studied adolescents and their childhood perceptions of parental alcoholism:

> At first they assumed that what they saw and experienced at home was normal; they had no way of knowing that other families were different. Their reality was not validated, and they grew up never being sure what to expect or what something meant. Praise, rules, and discipline were not consistent. Their parents' interaction with them was based on their current mood, the issue of the day, or the stage of intoxication of the alcoholic parent. They were lied to, abandoned, embarrassed, and abused. The secret of parental alcoholism surrounded them. It was not talked about inside the home, and outside the home the secret was well protected. (p. 527)

Children in an 80-proof home "live a game of 'let's pretend, let's protect', yet guarding the secret protects neither the alcoholic nor the children" (Seixas & Youcha, 1985, p. 4). The child's position is akin to Winnicott's concept of "false self," which Marla Morris (2009) explains is "someone who is so entangled in secrets that he doesn't even know who he is anymore. The reality principle cracks and utter confusion ensues" (p. 106). Children of Alcoholics, most assuredly entangled in secrets, have to create a false self. To the children, however, protecting the secret during the day is essential to the possibility of a peaceful night. Perhaps there will be less drama if the parent feels protected. Plus, children are told to obey their parents. So if Mama says, "Keep your mouth shut," that's what has to happen. There is a warped sense of what "right" and "wrong" mean in the household of a chronically drunk parent. It's right to lie. It's wrong to tell the truth. One must cover up. It's imperative to make excuses. Lie to avoid ambush from the outside. Lie to keep the beast breathing easily. Endeavor to convince people, yourself included, that all is normal on the home front. In their book about toxic parenting, Forward and Buck (1989) write:

> "The charade of the normal family" is especially damaging to a child because it forces him to deny the validity of his own feelings and perceptions. It is

almost impossible for a child to develop a strong sense of self-confidence if he must constantly lie about what he is thinking and feeling. (pp. 71–72)

A frighteningly extreme version of the need for secrets and cover-ups in alcoholic homes appears in MacCready's (2006) novel *Buried*. Claudine, a teenage girl who claims early on in the book that her mother is in rehab, pretends she is in constant touch with her mother in order to remain at home on her own. Claudine keeps the household going and attends school regularly. However, the girl becomes obsessive/compulsive. She leaves hundreds of sticky notes to herself all over the house, and continually organizes and reorganizes them. The reader is led to believe that the title references these sticky notes, which multiply daily at an alarming rate. Winnicott (1989c) explains that "an obsessional tendency may be organized to deal with confusion and to prevent the dangerous return of the destructive impulse" (p. 69). Claudine's obsession is clear, but what is not apparent is the destructive impulse she is trying to prevent from returning.

While the reader eventually realizes that Claudine's mother is not really in rehab, the mother's whereabouts are not clear until near the end, when the truth comes out. During the mother's last binge, Claudine finally "snapped" and fought back against the emotional abuse that had been hurled at her for years. She flung her drunk mother's empty beer bottles at the wall over her mother's head, and left her mother sobbing and pleading with Claudine not to leave. When Claudine returned home later, she found her mother dead from a head injury—one of the bottles had crashed *on* her mother's head, not above it. Horrified but afraid of going to jail, Claudine dragged her mother's body out to the garden and covered it with dirt. Therefore, during the entire time that she had been covering for her mother's absence, Claudine was just keeping one more family secret buried (MacCready, 2006).

AN AIR RAID A DAY

Parental battles can be hell enough when there is a second parent, and that parent does not abuse alcohol. However, if both parents are alcoholics, the fights are even more terrifying. My brother and I endured that situation when our mother married Derk, a man whose propensity for alcoholic rage was staggering. He brought three children of his own into the marriage, and we were expected to be one big happy family. In reality we were one big dysfunctional disaster. My mother's marriage to Derk was all about that fresh start. She was quite certain that everything would be "better" for us once they tied the knot. However, the knot became a noose, and the only fruits of her decision were years' worth of screaming, furniture breaking, and physical blows.

In my first foray into writing about the Geographic Cure (Nissen, 2006), I recalled the horrific fighting that went on between Marcia and Derk, which my mother endured for close to five years. Sometimes they fought in the open arena of the living room. However, it was the fighting behind the bedroom door that was the

CHAPTER 2

most terrifying, because we, the five blended-family siblings, could not see precisely what was happening. Lauretta Hannon (2009) describes a similar scenario from her own childhood: "They brawled behind closed doors, so the fights were an auditory experience, a sound track of horrors: yelling, furniture breaking, the thud of bodies slamming into walls and hitting the floor, grunts and sick laughs" (p. 26).

Hannon's and my experiences were not isolated incidents, by any means. Johnson (2001) reports, "Studies suggest that children in alcoholic families are more likely to experience verbal, physical, and sexual abuse and to witness verbal and physical violence between their parents than children in nonalcoholic families" (p. 134). Life with two alcohol-dependent, mercurial parents is doubly terrifying. Luckily the marriage between my mother and Derk self-destructed before one of them killed the other. My brother and I went back to being children of a single parent. There was a strangeness in being relieved of this return to "normal" (for us). However, Marcia's drinking took on entirely new dimensions once she was back on her own. Her propensity for volatile mothering climbed several notches higher.

While reading Christine Lawson's book, *The Borderline Mother* (2004), I realized that my alcoholic mother was a cross between two "borderline" categories: "Waif" and "Witch." Lawson explains that the Waif experiences "helplessness and hopelessness," and is "frequently victimized and evokes sympathy and concern from others" (p. 56). As if she had known my mother for years, Lawson writes about the Waif abandoning the very people she needs, discarding her friends, and grabbing "onto anything that might support her and keep her afloat" (p. 56). Reaching out for *the next better* is the Geographic Cure in a nutshell. Lawson's description of the Witch is an equally accurate description of one classic characteristic of chronically drunk parents:

> [A]ttacks by the Witch mother are unexpected and unpredictable . . . like tornadoes: random, devastating, and unpredictable. Naturally, her children are on constant alert for changes in the atmosphere that might indicate when and where she will "Turn." (p. 133)

This is a universal, daily event in the lives of Children of Alcoholics. Lawson's depiction of such a parental about-face is vivid:

> The Turn is a sudden attack, the abrupt withdrawal of love and affection, and razor-sharp words that can pierce at the heart as painfully as an arrow. . . . The disturbing reality is that the Turn may be triggered by circumstances that have nothing to do with the child. (p. 133)

When I first read this explanation of this "Turn" with a capital "T," I was struck by how accurately it described what went on in within our family's walls daily. The cycle became: sit on pins and needles waiting for the Turn, live through it, and then proceed directly to the dread stage once again. An alcoholic parent will "pull a 180" on others in a flash. Lawson (2004) tells precisely how children become "unconsciously preoccupied" with trying to ascertain the borderline mother's moods: "A fleeting glance, a furtive gesture, deceleration, and a shift of direction are signals of an approaching Turn" (p. 134). Children of Alcoholics who have alcoholic mothers or fathers have to pull round-the-clock duty, reading signals and adjusting accordingly. The inability to know what's coming next exhausts and defeats such children.

It is generally known that the most common characteristics of alcoholic homes are the factors of bedlam and unpredictability. As Gruber and Taylor (2006) explain, "Parental abuse of alcohol and other drugs can have a significant negative impact on a child. Young children may experience considerable difficulty comprehending changes in their parents' temperament or behavior when affected by alcohol and other drugs" (p. 13). Confusion is compounded for younger children because they have not yet identified the triggers that set off the parent. Even if a Child of an Alcoholic eventually sees the source of fermented parenting as a disease, the only gain is an understanding of terms. "Children may name and understand the alcohol abuse but still perceive the situation as uncontrollable" (Haugland, 2005, p. 238). Additionally, identifying alcohol as the perpetrator of abusive parenting does little for the child in improving his or her relations with the drunk parent. The child does not understand why dad or mom can't just leave alcohol alone. The perceived clear choice—*the bottle or me*—leaves the child standing there with the short end of the stick.

Children of Alcoholics are experts in waiting for the other shoe to drop. Just when they think they have the fine distinctions of the parent's moods figured out, everything changes once again. Robinson and Rhoden (1998) describe the typical randomness of life in an alcoholic home:

> Alcoholics are notorious for mood swings and making and breaking promises during drinking bouts. . . . In some ways this predicament is like living in schizophrenia, where parental mood swings are unpredictable and expectations are inconsistent. Children often find themselves walking on eggshells and desperately trying to second-guess parents in order to do what they want. (pp. 62–63)

To grow up in this chaotic manner is to also doubt, on a daily basis, one's own ability to understand what's going on right in front of you. Torchia (2003) notes that "a child, even a young child, tries to make sense of a situation, [and] is confused when the parent's behavior makes no sense" (p. 1). This is one of many reasons why, early on, the Child of an Alcoholic learns to mistrust everyone, including herself. Killeen (1988) illustrates this trust issue:

> In an atmosphere where clear evidence of alcoholic behavior is denied and labeled as rational behavior, children learn that they cannot trust their own perceptions. The cognitive and emotional consequences are confusion, an inability to test reality, and the absence of a secure sense of their strengths and abilities. (p. 27)

Treading lightly and remaining insecure every waking hour is a miserable and demoralizing modus operandi for the Child of an Alcoholic, but there is little

CHAPTER 2

choice in the matter. A second, non-addicted parent in the home may try to buffer the situation for young Children of Alcoholics, as do older siblings. However, the damage is still far-reaching. Buffers, too, have to tiptoe around the drinker to avoid an uprising. O'Rourke (1990) explains:

> When entire families organize themselves around the behavior of an alcoholic, individuals are continually kept off balance while anticipating drinking behaviors that are entirely unpredictable. . . . The young child may view the alcoholic parent as two different people, one good and one bad. . . . Most are angry at some level that the sober parent cannot make things any better. (p. 107)

Ironically, young Children of Alcoholics do not even know that their situation is not normal. They have no idea that life is different in other homes. In my case, I thought that all kids had to tell their mothers that it was time to go to bed. I assumed it was children's responsibility to put cigarettes out, put milk bottles outside the door, lock doors, and turn off lights. As I understood it, my mother's mood of the moment was my responsibility to decipher. Life for Children of Alcoholics means immersion in the *unsaid*. Once children realize they are growing up in fermented homes they want desperately to tell someone, but, even more desperately, they want to keep things at home on an even keel. At all costs they avoid rocking the boat.

Walking on eggshells every day is depressing, and depression is common in Children of Alcoholics. They "often live with pervasive tension and stress, have higher levels of anxiety and depression, do poorly in school, and experience problems with coping" (U.S. Dept. of HHS, SAMHSA, 2007). The old phrase about tension being "thick enough to cut with a knife" has never rung more true than it does when describing the home of a drunken parent. Middleton-Moz and Dwindle (1986) note an analogy made by psychiatrist George Vaillant, who stated that "often, living with alcoholism is second only in stress to being in prisoner camps in World War II" (p. 227). To clarify the comparison, Middleton-Moz and Dwindle describe the acutely stressful life of a Child of an Alcoholic: "When an individual lives with an air raid a day, chronic stress becomes normal. . . . The child survives through the use of denial, hypervigilance, and psychic numbing" (p. 227).

When Children of Alcoholics are very young, they suffer from wild confusion. When they're older, they suffer from hatred of the very people they're expected to love. They know they are expected to honor their chronically inebriated mother or father. Alice Miller (2005) describes this confusing imperative:

> On closer inspection, however, we see that the Fourth Commandment contains a threat, a kind of moral blackmail that has lost none of its potency: If you want to live a long life, you have to honor your parent, even if they do not deserve it; otherwise you will die an early death. (p. 26)

One of the most difficult hurdles of surviving the 80-proof home is deciding that it's acceptable to be angry with your besotted parent, because the relational dynamic between parent and child is wrecked. Damage becomes the household standard. Ultimately, Children of Alcoholics find that, as Michael Eigen (2005b) describes, relationships "do not feel real without damage" (p. 13). What a legacy to carry into one's adult life! (This is a primary reason why there are support groups all over the country for Adult Children of Alcoholics.)

Chaos and damage are the guiding parent-child relational forces in the novel mentioned earlier in this chapter, *Buried*. Claudine, the central character, belongs to a Teens of Alcoholics group, which often discuss the unpredictability of life at home. She tells the group:

> It's like after a big fight and you've made up. Things are balanced just so, but you haven't really talked it out. You think it's all fine again because it looks good on the outside, but things can only last so long that way before, BAM! You have to deal with it all again. . . . It's what Matt said. . . . You know something worse is coming. (MacCready, 2006, p. 96)

Shifts are continuous in homes where random life prevails. Ballard and Cummings (1990) have described alcoholic homes as chaotic, unpredictable, and chronically inconsistent in all the usual familial aspects, which makes normal child development a hit-or-miss operation. The child internalizes and feels responsible for everything that seems amiss about the mood of the hour. The confusion for a young child is especially prominent, and there are heavy-laden feelings of inadequacy. A Child of an Alcoholic feels that he is constantly doing something "wrong." Ruben (2001) explains what is commonly reported by Adult Children of Alcoholics about their childhoods:

> Children of Alcoholics most often come from homes where rules are subject to the whim of the person in the room at the time. Children of Alcoholics may have been ordered to do one thing by a father, forbidden to do the same thing by a mother, told to do it differently by a grandparent, and ridiculed for doing it (or not doing it) by an uncle or friends of the family. As a result, Children of Alcoholics grow up hearing they can never do anything right; they are somehow defective. (p. 8)

Of all the perilous moments in a Child of an Alcoholic's daily life, few are more frightening than the span of time, however fleeting, when the drunk parent cannot be woken up. Regardless of how accustomed one becomes to the routine, it is nevertheless heart stopping, especially for young children. I hated that "oh my God" moment that remained suspended in the air, timeless, until my mother's grunts sounded the all-is-well. Christensen (1997) writes, "Daily life involves a great deal of emotional stress for these children. Children are afraid of being abandoned. They are afraid that their parents will die (they may have seen them appear lifeless)" (p. 29). Finding my mother dead would frankly not have surprised me. In my later teen years I would have been convinced that suicide, rather than an accidental overdose, was what killed her. Marcia would not have been the first alcoholic to decide that suicide was the solution to "painful resolutions and shattering failures of sobriety," as Kirsch (2005, p. 150) phrases it. She indoctrinated me to expect it, even when referring to suicide in veiled terms. The combination of depression and habitual alcohol consumption "often leads to suicidal behavior," notes Sher (2006), who states that "Individuals with alcohol dependence have a 60–120 times greater suicide risk than the non-psychiatrically-ill population" (p. 59).

I was never certain of the degree to which Marcia's allusions to suicide qualified as *risk*, as compared to *drama*. When I was young, Marcia's dramatic, "Soon you won't have to worry about me ever again" declarations rattled me to pieces. She would wake me up deep into the night to slur her way through such announcements, waiting for me to say, "Don't say that!" In school the next day, I would be consumed with worry and sleepiness. I spent many school hours wondering if she'd actually make good on her threats. It's difficult to concentrate on the water cycle during a science lesson when it's raining bourbon at home. As I advanced through middle and high school, however, the threat rolled off my back like spring rain. At 12 years old, I muffled, "Go ahead!" into a pillow and then felt exceedingly guilty for having such a thought. At 16, I said it to my mother's face and convinced myself I meant it. How unnerving to wish that a parent would stop beating around the bush and just end it all. As far as I was concerned, I was raising Geoff anyway, so what would be the difference? More often, though, I simply calculated when it would be possible to grab Geoff and leave. It is intriguing to me that the option I considered to be the most viable solution to my troubles was to *run* the minute I turned 18. The Geographic Cure gene had certainly passed from mother to daughter.

For many of the millions of children who are subjected to fermented parenting, nights and weekends are ruled by relentless pandemonium, secret guarding, and parentification. In contrast, their daytime classrooms have the potential to be places where they can revel in warmth and stability, or at least, just breathe evenly, regularly, for a while. Yet, tragically, teachers don't have time to figure out how to build a relationship with their students. Teachers can't contemplate or discuss with colleagues the particular needs of Children of Alcoholics, nor their students living in trauma, because they're too engulfed in the flames of their own disordered environment at work. Many teachers dwell in a contrary hell of their own: the grasping-at-straws frenzy of accountability, standards, the newest of new teacher evaluation programs, and mandated testing. No wonder Children of Alcoholics are often neglected at school as well (and they aren't the only ones). No one at school has time for them.

CHAPTER 3

THE UNHINGED LIVES OF KIDS ON THE MOVE

INSET: RINGO, SHUT UP!

In the middle of my fourth-grade year, we moved to a large apartment complex on top of a hill in Huntsville, Alabama. This was the second of three moves within one city, crossing school zone boundaries each time. I was the new kid yet again, but I quickly discovered that two of my classmates, Kiki and Liza, lived in my same apartment complex. The three of us bonded over our true and infinite love for the Beatles. I relished being part of a group of "real" friends—true friends—talking and laughing at lunch and on the school bus every day. The experience was brand new for me.

Once we arrived home, however, we usually had to part ways. Kiki and Liza were allowed to roam the grounds of the complex, pool, and hillside with other kids after school. My little brother's babysitter was only paid to stay with him until I got home from school, so I could never join my friends. The girls would come to the door asking me to play, and I would turn them down each time, explaining that I was babysitting Geoff. When they asked why the babysitter didn't stay, I told them that she wasn't needed; I was "in charge" until my mother came home from work.

When summer arrived, I became my brother's full-time babysitter. I was loving life in those days because I held in my hot little hand a ticket to go see the Beatles in Atlanta. Miss Kelly, Kiki's mother, bought tickets for our group as a present for her daughter. The plan was that she would take us to the August concert via Greyhound, and we would spend the night in Atlanta. Birthday money from Dad would cover my share of the bus fare, hotel room, and food. I was astounded that my mother gave me permission to go. For hours I would stare at photo of the Fab Four on my ticket, barely believing I would soon see them in person.

A week before the event, Marcia abruptly made me give the ticket back. The weekend had been a particularly saturated one, and her disposition was venomous. Apparently at some point I snapped at my mother about something trivial. She didn't like my tone and launched into a staggering tirade about what a smart-ass I had become. I was commanded to take the ticket back immediately so that Kiki's mother could find someone who *deserved* to go. My sobbing made no difference. Marcia would not even let me wait until the next day to return the ticket. (I was hoping she would see things differently, once sober.)

When I found Miss Kelly, I tried to concoct a ridiculous story about a conflict with our summer plans. However, my friend's mother had already guessed what the score was in our household. This incident confirmed her suspicions. She gave me a hug

CHAPTER 3

while she pried the ticket out of my reluctant hand. When Miss Kelly subsequently told her husband what happened, Kiki was within earshot. She told Liza, and then together they told all the other kids in the complex that I wasn't going to the concert because of my drunk mother. They were already choosing another girl to go. When one of the other kids came to tell me this, I was crushed down to a nub. So much for the novel experience of making "true" friends in our newest, for-sure-better place.

When my mother returned to work that Monday, I stewed and fumed, playing my Beatles albums on full volume, startling my brother. A few times during the course of the day Kiki and Liza used our group's secret knock at my door, but I ignored them. I hated life.

On Tuesday I had a brainstorm. A wild rumor had been circulating all summer, claiming that the Beatles liked to stay in private homes while touring in order to avoid the press. Not only would they stay with fans, the rumor elaborated, but the Fab Four might even go to a completely different city, to throw off the photographers and fans, and then take a helicopter to their concert venue. Every kid in our area knew about the rumor; we had been crazy with speculation. Huntsville would be the perfect hiding place for "our boys" before their Atlanta concert.

My demented idea took shape as the stereo blasted away, and then I heard the knock again. In a pseudo-hushed tone, I demanded, "Stop! You have to hide!" and then pulled the stereo needle straight up from the record, so there would be no scratching sounds. I banged a few chairs into each other and slammed the coat closet door. Then I opened the front door just a crack and peeked out. Kiki and Liza stood together, perplexed.

"What do you want?" I asked them, doing my best to appear guarded and nervous. I kept glancing over one shoulder and frowning at air.

"What are you doing in there?" Kiki asked, contorting herself with attempts peer inside.

"Nothing," I told her. "I really have to go. Can't talk. Bye!"

I slammed the door and then banged more chairs around, opened the closet door, and started the music back up. Two minutes later I heard a pounding version of the secret knock. I went through the same routine again, pulling the needle back up, shushing, then whisper-yelling, "Paul, go in the kitchen! George, move over! Ringo, shut *up!*" I was so wildly into this charade that my adrenaline was pumping like a river dredge. My clattering and banging sounds were disgracefully loud. This time when I cracked opened the door, I saw two other kids with Kiki and Liza. Again I claimed to be far too busy to talk. When they asked once more what I was doing, I told them that I was rearranging furniture. Their young minds were as gullible as mine was deranged. Their faces said it all: *Could it be?* My wounded nine-year-old soul relished the fact that Kiki and Liza thought the Beatles were in my apartment. My scheme seemed like a perfectly natural way to turn my *un*true friends into the girls who felt excluded.

Not too long after Kiki and Liza saw the Beatles without me, my mother wrote a remorseful letter to me saying how sorry she was about the ticket incident, and how she was going to "get better this time for sure." Her closing line was, "I just need to start over." That, of course, meant another move would soon come creeping around the corner.

FAMILIES UNMOORED

> The challenge is complicated because new students bring educational histories and knowledge of subject matter that do not always match the shared experiences of the classes they enter.
> —Andrea A. Lasch and Sandra L. Kirkpatrick, *A Classroom Perspective on Student Mobility*

> Ultimately, cultural difference is read by teachers as deprivation.
> —Judith Remy Leder, *Conclusion: Whither Changing Schools?*

In the last 20 years, high rates of family mobility have been shown in research to be clearly problematic for the school-aged children involved. Such children, considered "highly mobile" or "transient" students, often enter their new schools with myriad social, emotional, and academic adjustment problems that have been observed in the U.S. as well as other countries (Bainbridge, 2003; Bartolomeo, 2006; Chao & Clements, 2005; Franke, Isken, & Parra, 2003; Gruman, Harachi, Abbott, Catalano & Fleming, 2008; Hango, 2006; Hall, 2001; Jacobson, 2001; Jensen, 2009; Kerbow, 1996; Lasch & Kirkpatrick, 1990; Maxwell, 2008; Million, 2000; *New Zealand Herald*, 2005; NACOA, n.d.; Offenberg, 2004; Smith, Fien, & Paine, 2008; Strand & Demie, 2007). Elevated family mobility rates and the related stressors for school-aged children are *part* of the formula that makes Geographic Cure Children unique. In this chapter I explore transiency alone, and then bring mobility and parental alcoholism together in Chapter 4.

As a highly mobile child I certainly experienced many layers of emotional, social, and academic problems related to our frequent moves. When I made friends, I soon had to leave them behind, and the pain of breaking those ties grew more intense each time. When, proactively, I did not attempt to make friends, I was exceedingly lonely. If I tried to be outgoing, I felt foolish. If I remained quiet, I was viewed as "stuck up." Every time we moved I tried to reinvent a better version of myself, but insecurities prevailed. As Eigen (2005a) states, "It is not possible to grow another personality from scratch. One is stuck with oneself. Yet one can dip into the storehouse of possibilities, shift attitudes, and rework one's sense of what it means to be an experiencing subject" (pp. 265–266). The Life Erratic presents numerous opportunities for mobile children to regroup, whether those options are welcome or not.

Weissbourd (1996) explains that frequent relocations are just as traumatic for children as are other difficulties that may have higher profiles:

> Children from poor and single-parent families in particular are driven from place to place by troubles. . . . Compared with other problems of childhood,

such as violence and single parenthood, repeated moving has received little attention—it is often not considered a problem at all. Yet repeated moving may be just as damaging as the more often acknowledged problems. (p. 106)

Poverty and single-parenthood are the two most prevalent common denominators of highly mobile families. Like Weissbourd, Wood et al. (1993) found that children from families living below the poverty line and with a single parent (or grandparent) were more likely to move repeatedly; the same was true of children whose parents were unemployed, had obtained less than a high school education, and/or whose mother was younger than 18 years when the child was born. The odds are stacked against such parents who may be trying everything in their power to keep the family afloat. And there are indeed parents who fight to pull themselves and their kids out of dire circumstances. I have taught their children and have seen for myself how ferociously parents will fight to keep their kids together under one roof, even when the rooftop constantly changes.

Children living in dismal situations have to create for themselves a way to preserve some semblance of equilibrium amidst the chaos. Anna Freud (1936/1961) explains that defense mechanisms "are designed to secure the ego and to save it from experiencing 'pain'" (p. 4). My defenses remained on high alert, day in and day out. In an effort to avoid pain, I utilized humor routinely, finding something funny about much that was going on around me. Later, as my little brother grew old enough to polish his own "funny side" to a shine, I had a co-conspirator for life. Humor, explains Grostein (1999), "is the other side of feeling sorry for oneself" (p. 72).

Emotional damage in highly mobile children is no small issue. Weissbourd (1996) explains that perpetual mobility "can deprive children of nearly all the ingredients of sturdy growth, creating stresses on parents that impair parenting, robbing children of opportunities for lasting achievement, and hindering children's ability to draw on friends and community adults" (pp. 106–107). Children who move frequently are solitary children, experiencing only sprinkles of friendship with other children their own age and few sustained adult interactions, if any. They have only minimal opportunities for healthy relationships. When children are uprooted from family members, familiar neighbors, and friends, the lack of relationships hits hard. Children who have remained in one neighborhood for a while may be much more confident about their surroundings, because there are people nearby who can be trusted. Kullman (2010) notes that "trust is a central affect in growing up, as it encourages children to explore spaces further afield" (p. 836). Children who trust the familiarity of their surroundings know that they may always return back without harm. Conversely, children for whom surroundings often change have no such trust in place.

Although family transiency is nothing new, Franke et al. (2003) state that "only recently has the transient urban school-age child received the attention by researchers, educators, and policy makers that is merited" (p. 150). One might hope that this additional attention paid to transiency was prompted by genuine concern for transient children. Unfortunately, however, school accountability is more likely the impetus behind this newfound interest. Policy makers are realizing that mobility affects test scores (Viadero, 2009). I agree that transient school-aged children indeed present problems that should be carefully considered by educators and policy makers, but it is not Adequate Yearly Progress that concerns me. Rather, it is concern for the highly mobile children's care that should drive our research, responsive teaching, and policy decisions.

When a child is taken, mid-year, to a new teacher's classroom door, the teacher can either deliver a crushing blow, or she can support the child for whatever short period of time the "new kid" is in her charge. On numerous occasions in my career I have seen, first-hand, a teacher's reaction to having a new child brought to her door—they often say something like this: "Oh, terrific. You've got to be kidding me—another kid? I don't even have another desk in here!" or "Does Mr. Z. not remember that I already have 27 students? He must have it out for me." *This* with the new child standing right there. However, I feel that, in many cases, it is not necessarily an uncaring heart that prompts such a response, but panic about student performance, test scores, and how the class will match up to the others on that grade level when the "data wall" charts are posted. Perhaps this is why, among commonly recognized student mobility problems such as difficulty in obtaining student records, *teacher attitudes* about highly mobile students also tops the list (Bainbridge, 2003; Knight et al., 1992; Million, 2000). Mobility has a marked impact upon teachers and school staff as students move from one school to the other, and this is far from a rare occurrence. For but one example, Bainbridge (2003) reports that "on average, one in three students in the Columbus Public School System changes schools each year" (p. 2).

This issue is prominent not only in the U.S., but globally as well. The *New Zealand Herald* (2005) reported two of that country's most extreme cases of transiency, involving "a nine-year-old Hokianga boy who has attended 13 schools and a five-year-old Whangarei boy who has been sent to three schools in a month" (p. 1). Student mobility concerns have been recently addressed in Canada by Hango (2006); in the U.K. by Strand and Demie (2007); in Norway by Jensen (2009); and in Scotland by the *Times Educational Supplement* (May 22, 2009). In a book entitled *Traveller, Nomadic, and Migrant Education* (2009), editors Danaher, Kenny, and Leder included articles about transient children in Italy, Scotland, Australia, England, Russia, India, and several other countries. There are children in all parts of the world who are coping with problems related to being "the new kid" on a continuing basis. Meanwhile, school staff, perplexed, wonder how to "deal" with them. Little if any attention is paid to issues surrounding highly mobile children in most teacher preparation and inservice programs. There is a central assumption built in to most classroom instruction and management lore that once the first few days of school have passed, the class rolls remain stable for the year. However, "this assumption of stability is inappropriate for many schools. Students do move, and they move at all times during the year" (Lasch & Kirkpatrick, 1990, p. 190).

CHAPTER 3

Without a doubt, mobility is woven into the fabric of modern life. One report on mobile elementary children indicated that "approximately 17% of U.S. third-graders (more than 500,000 children) have attended at least three different schools since starting first grade" (Sanderson, 2003, p. 601). Unfortunately even one family move can create emotional problems in very young children, as the American Academy of Child and Adolescent Psychiatry (AACAP, 2011) points out:

> Children in kindergarten or first grade may be particularly vulnerable to a family move because developmentally they are just in the process of separating from their parents and adjusting to new authority figures and social relationships. The relocation can interfere with that normal process of separation by causing them to return to a more dependent relationship with their parents. (p. 1)

Regardless of their ages, children whose families move multiple times are vulnerable to a host of anxiety and stress-related difficulties even without school factoring into the equation. To their parents, frequent moves are deemed necessary to solve pressing issues too large or uncontrollable to face. However, kids are perceptive. They compare their situations with other children who move, and they notice that when family relocation is related to a parent's job transfer, military assignment, higher education pursuits, or other reasons perceived as legitimate or "honorable," the move may be painful, but there is no sense of panic in the air. The adults in those cases don't seem to be floundering. In fact, the concepts of "moving up" or being adventurous are considered part of the American Way:

> Equating family moves with individual betterment and social improvement is deeply embedded in the American ethos. . . . Maxims such as "Go West, young man" glorified relocation as a characteristic of success and social improvement. However, the history of family relocation in the United States also has a shadow side. (Wood et al., 1993, p. 1334)

When frequent moves are the norm, and when they are initiated as a next-desperate-measure, the "shadow side" of relocation indeed rears its ugly head, to be sure. Children bear the weight of such measures, and carry that burden with them when they walk into teachers' classrooms. Since, in far too many cases, teachers "regard differences among students as deficits that need to be corrected" (Leder, 2009, p. 215), they see their work as doubled, even tripled, with the child who enters mid-year.

After being "in the classroom" for nearly 25 years, I accepted a system-level position in the area of professional learning. I trained hundreds of new teachers each year as part of our system's orientation and induction programs, and I coached dozens of struggling new teachers individually. Some were assigned to me because their principals put them on a "professional development plan," and others voluntarily asked for assistance. Additionally, I trained hundreds of veteran teachers in professional development courses on data analysis, professional learning communities, the Next Better Teaching Strategy, and so on. The county would pay some out-of-town "expert" thousands of dollars to come to our district to train trainers, who were then expected to pass on the torch of New and Better to their schools. I was often called upon to be a torch-carrier. I couldn't do it for long. I loved interacting with teachers. I did *not* love my role as a school system "company girl." After the third year I bailed on my colleagues and went back into a school. I could no longer look classroom teachers in the eye and say that the rabid demands placed upon them in the name of standards and accountability were worthwhile.

I bring up this career experience to point out that when I write about my informal observations of and conversations with classroom teachers, I am not referring to two teachers on my hallway. Instead, I am referring to hundreds of elementary, middle, and high school teachers who were new, veteran, and international (new to the U.S. schools). No matter what the original purposes of the training and peer coaching sessions were, our discussions always came around to what was most frustrating for the teachers. Consistently, a major source of frustration expressed to me by teachers at all K-12 levels was the high incidence of student mobility.

Revolving classroom doors will often throw a monkey wrench into teachers' attempts to put into action the strategies they are expected to implement. They frankly do not know what to do with transient children when they have already trained other students to jump through the newest standardized hoops. Padfield and Cameron (2009) report, "Anecdotal evidence suggests that schools are less than confident in responding to the unexpected arrival of Traveller-children and in responding to mobile children's learning needs" (p. 33). On a good day, they're less than confident. In my observations, I've seen that they are more often aggravated, resentful, and exasperated. This is not because such teachers are uncaring people. They are just at their wits' end, and the specter of accountability hovers nearby, always.

As I mentioned earlier, teacher preparation courses do not usually figure high mobility rates into the equation, and neither do the inservice trainings that teachers are mandated to attend. Teachers are expected to build a sense of community in the class and yet they are also ordered to be on the right page at the right time when the "classroom walk-throughs" take place. They will be held responsible for the scores their students make on standardized benchmark and achievement tests. Therefore, when a new student is brought to their class far into the school year, the most typical reaction is dismay. Some hide their consternation well; others do not. Perhaps some teachers feel that mobile children add just one more layer to an impossible job. Shoshana Felman (1997) writes about the consideration of teaching as "impossible":

> If teaching is impossible—as Freud and Socrates both point out—what are we teachers doing? How should we understand—and carry out—our task? . . . It is my contention . . . that it is precisely in giving us unprecedented insight into the impossibility of teaching, that psychoanalysis has opened up unprecedented teaching possibilities, renewing both the questions and the practice of education. (p. 18)

CHAPTER 3

The questions I ask are: Whose interests are being served by the business model and the bottom-line mentality that drive education? How long will it take for all "stakeholders" to see that we are being driven right off a cliff? What does the worship of standardization do to children who must attend schools under such mentally exhausting conditions? And most of all, how can teachers engage in meaningful dialogue with children who tumble in mid-year, and who likely won't remain for long? I encourage teachers to try, even if to do so means to stray from the daily plan. That one measure of consideration might make a drastic difference in a transient child's hectic life. Many teachers and administrators cannot fathom the trials that such children have experienced, and that needs to change. I am asking educators to seek to know more about mobile children because the bottom line is that transient students abound in our schools. The frequency of student mobility is only going to increase.

One significant way to familiarize educators with the ordeals that mobile children endure could be through literature—biography, memoir, fiction, and juvenile fiction. In my research I had hopes of finding stories about children who move frequently; I thought that such stories would enlighten teachers and perhaps lead them to add such books to their classroom libraries. I searched for children's books that specifically tackle the issue of frequent moves and school changes. Unfortunately, I found that the available literature comes up short. For the most part, the books about moving that do exist are geared toward young children, and address an isolated incidence of a family move for a logical reason, such as dad's new job. Many are written in a blatantly syrupy "Let's take this lemon and make lemonade!" tone, which frankly made me toss them aside. Highly mobile children would greatly benefit from realistic stories about children who share their plight, and educators would learn much from such stories as well. The children's fiction sections of most bookstores include several great books about children who live with alcoholic parents. My hope is that mobility as a theme will catch up soon.

TRANSIENT STUDENTS TYPICALLY DEFINED

> At that point the Carrey family saga took an even more bizarre twist. Having no other roof over their heads, Percy, Kay, John, Rita and Jim moved into a beat-up yellow Volkswagen camper van. For eight months, they called that van home, parking it on campgrounds in the Toronto area.
> —Martin Knelman, *Jim Carrey: The Joker is Wild*

> My dad is packing. My mom is packing. My brothers Nick and Anthony are packing. I'm not packing. I'm not going to move.
> —Judith Viorst, *Alexander, Who's Not (Do You Hear Me? I Mean It!) Going to Move*

For many, the terms "transient" or "highly mobile" bring to mind children who are on the move due to military, migrant, or homeless circumstances. Transient students from military families "move about three times as often as most American families," Bartolomeo (2006) reports, adding that there are "more than one million military children in U.S. public schools, and many move 10 or more times before graduating from high school" (p. 45). In a stunning novel entitled, *As the Crow Flies,* MacDonald (2004) describes what it's like to be a military child:

> If your father is in the air force, people ask you where you are from and it's difficult to answer. The answer becomes longer the older you get, because you move every few years. "Where are you from?" "I'm from the Royal Canadian Air Force." The RCAF. Like a country whose bits are scattered around the globe. (p. 12)

In *When Mom's a Marine*, Bartolomeo (2006) addresses particular issues facing military children in regard to frequent changes of school. The author quotes a math and chemistry teacher with 37 years of experience in the classroom, who stated that some teachers consider military children to be "just passing through. These kids face the same challenges the rest of their peers do—insecurity, peer pressure, trying to fit in. . . . [I]t's very stressful, especially if the parent is in a combat zone" (Bartolomeo, p. 45). No doubt there are significant stressors of enormous magnitude for military children to bear.

However, I contend that the mobility of military families, while frequent, is not usually based on inebriated parental decisions made on the spur of the moment. Therefore I do not consider this circumstance of relocation to be part of the Geographic Cure. Most assignments result in military families remaining in place for at least two years, and notice is given when the time comes to move again. Additionally, there is a supportive and shared culture on base and in the military communities that helps family members adjust:

> Each bit, each base, looks like every other, so there is a consistency to this nation. Like walking into any Catholic church and hearing the Latin Mass, you can go to a base—station, that is—anywhere in the world and understand it. (MacDonald, 2004, p. 12)

Weissbourd (1996) notes that Army psychologists are available for help with adjustment issues, and the Army makes a point of recommending that "parents and professionals can help children in supplying elements of predictability—by letting children know well in advance when a move is going to occur and describing what the new place will be like" (p. 110). For the students who are Geographic Cure Children, however, the only element of predictability is that more random moves are likely on the horizon.

The special needs of migrant children create another set of possible stressors, which I, again, see as a separate case from Geographic Cure Children. "Nearly 400,000 students whose families have moved back and forth between Mexico and the United States in the past three years to secure agricultural jobs are being served by U.S. schools," Zehr (2006) writes, adding that this situation prompted

CHAPTER 3

a joint venture "between state and federal education officials and Mexico" to send exchange teachers across the border between the U.S. and Mexico (p. 16). Typically there are high numbers of migrant students who do not finish high school, but there are difficulties in studying the obstacles those students face because the students themselves are hard to track (Gibson & Hidalgo, 2009). However, I contend that, as with military families, there is to some extent a supportive culture within migrant worker communities and the schools that serve them. The children are not as likely to feel at odds with their classmates because many of their peers are in similar situations. Plus, family moves are related to seasonal jobs for the parents. A child can see the logic behind such a move, which is not the case when a family is relocated based on a random, rash decisions made after a binge-drinking marathon.

Homeless children and Geographic Cure Children do have some common experiences. It is extremely difficult to track homeless and highly mobile children who move in and out of shelters; therefore, it is also hard to offer them consistent services. Peter Miller (2009) suggests that now that the McKinney-Vento Homeless Assistance Act (as reauthorized in 2001) defines homeless children and youth as "individuals who lack a fixed, regular and adequate nighttime residence," the U.S. must redefine homeless education "as a practice that is to be engaged by a multitude of institutions and individuals" (p. 617). Some schools are surprised to learn that, indeed, there are homeless children on their class rolls. One Maryland school received their wake-up call a few years ago. "Charles County is not poor. In fact, Forbes magazine listed it as the 20th richest county in America in 2008," states Hardy (2009), and yet, "since 2007, the number of homeless students in Charles County has grown more than 50 percent" (p. 18). There are indeed homeless parents whose financial circumstances are devastating, but they are not necessarily alcoholics, nor are they addicted to other drugs. (To assume that all homeless people are addicts of some type is to be clueless about the reality of homelessness.) I assert that homeless children, also, should not be considered Geographic Cure Children based on their living situation alone.

Military, migrant, and homeless children *may* also be living with a parent who is an escape artist and may indeed shoulder the role of a Geographic Cure Child, in addition to having other circumstances involved. However, my assignation of the term Geographic Cure Children is based upon an alcoholic parent's decision to relocate (for possibly the fourth time in a year) being the result of a whim. There is no long-term planning. It's simply time to move (again) because when everything is better, *then* he or she will stop drinking. Alcoholism *and* running off randomly, to the elusive fresh start, are implicated. Transient students, however, are typically defined as students who change schools with great frequency, period. For this purposes of this chapter, I am exploring transiency alone.

As mobile children, my brother and I were never totally homeless or destitute, but we came alarmingly close. My mother did manage to find a new job each time she lost or left one, even if it took a while, and my father sent child support checks. We lived in apartments or rental homes that alternated between "shabby" and "disgusting." The only time we lived in a nice house was when Marcia nabbed a husband and we became, for a time, an instant Brady Bunch family, moving to another state before taking up the new quarters. The minute that calamity ended my family was back in a low-rent apartment complex once more. Soon after, we were crossing state lines yet again, heading off to encroach upon an aunt for a while. Highly mobile families often move in and out of relatives' homes, and we were no exception. When there was no money for rent we mooched off of aunts, uncles, and our grandmother. I was not aware of the term "transient student," but on most days I detested being one. I didn't meet many other children who were "the new kid all the time," as I was. When I was very young I thought it was par for the course to move often. By the time I was 11 years old, I was sick of moving. *The Slums of Beverly Hills* (Nozik & Wlodkowski, 1998), a comedy film about a dysfunctional family, set in the late 1970s, portrays a frequently mobile family. Murray, a lower-middle-class father of three who is estranged from his wife, moves his children every few months from one cheap apartment to another, usually because the past-due rent catches up with him. The movie is hilarious (in large part due to the family dynamics), but as the film entertains, it also does an excellent job of illustrating the angst felt by kids who are frequently uprooted with no notice.

Through the process of *currere* I have come to think reflectively about this transient childhood of mine, and how my experiences in that era frame not only my personal relationships today, but my pedagogical ones as well. Those experiences also frame this book, as mobility is a major component of the Geographic Cure. In light of my strong feelings about this topic, my study may be considered by some as subjective. However in the field of curriculum studies, there is a place for topics about which writers feel strongly, even though such was not always the case. Madeleine Grumet (2006) recalls earlier curriculum studies days when subjectivity was considered trivial, and when children were left out of the research and analysis equation:

> If you attended the meeting of the American Educational Research Association in those days you rarely heard children mentioned in discussion of curriculum theory. No one ever confessed to having been a child, and in presentations no one even admitted knowing a child. Of course, if you spent time in the coffee shops, all your colleagues ever talked about were their children: over breakfast, over coffee, over lunch, over dinner, at table after table after table. (p. 208)

Two of the theoretical questions Grumet (2006) investigated during those early days of curriculum studies were: "What did it mean to have been children?" and "How did the experiences of having been children and parents influence the education we constructed for other people's children?" (p. 208). Through this book I am exploring questions about children as well. I certainly am becoming more aware of how my experiences as a child on the move have framed, and continue to frame, the education I construct for children now.

CHAPTER 3

The child who is on the move is one who rarely manages to adjust to school as expected. For such a student, school-related learning is a haphazard undertaking at best. Being the new kid on a continual basis is overwhelmingly stressful. "Changing schools is almost certain to disrupt, to some extent, a child's learning experience," writes Kerbow (1996, p. 158), and if this disruption happens chronically, major stressors arise. In an article aptly titled "Moving Targets," Jacobson (2001) reports observing a school guidance counselor who compared student stressors associated with moving to the grieving process. When turmoil surrounds the move, anxiety levels can climb even higher for the children involved, but they often internalize their traumatized feelings:

> Some youngsters may not talk about their distress, so parents should be aware of the warning signs of depression, including changes in appetite, social withdrawal, a drop in grades, irritability, sleep disturbances or other dramatic changes in behavior or mood. . . . Children who seem depressed by a move may be reacting more to the stress they are experiencing than to the relocation. Sometimes one parent may be against the move, and children will sense and react to this parental discord. (AACAP, 2011, p. 1)

When a child displays these signs of depression in school, he or she can cause aggravated reactions from a teacher who has no clue about the child's devastation. Negative reactions from the teacher then add to the child's anxiety levels. I have a vivid memory of having a letter jerked away from me that I was writing to a friend I'd made in a previous school. I was finished with the vocabulary worksheet assigned, so I decided to pull out my three-ring binder and pour my heart out to the friend. The teacher, Ms. Baja, snatched the letter right out of the binder, admonishing me about "rushing" to complete the assignment before even looking to see that my answers were correct. Ms. Baja had no concept of my sense of loss or my anxiety, or how often I experienced those feelings renewed. John Dewey (1938/1977) insisted that an educator needs "that sympathetic understanding of individuals as individuals which gives him an idea of what is actually going on in the minds of those who are learning" (p. 39). However, my teacher had no idea what was going on with me, nor did she venture to guess. When I received a grade of "100" for the worksheet, she still refused to give the letter back to me. Ms. Baja insisted I complete more worksheets to "catch up" on what the class was working on before my arrival. She needed grades to put in her roll book for me, and to make sure we were all on the same page. For many years I've observed, as a mobile student and as an educator, that the puzzle of student mobility that garners teachers' attention the most is *their own* problems coping with it.

THE LONG, LOUD SIGH: STUDENT MOBILITY FROM THE SCHOOL PERSPECTIVE

Before long I was recounting life on the road with my father, including the fact that, despite my now being an academic of some distinction, I hardly ever attended school, missing some grades entirely and never reaching beyond the first weeks of high school.

—Michael Keith, *The Next Better Place*

Sanderson (2003) reports on the results of a teacher survey that revealed teachers' concerns about highly mobile children:

> Teachers frequently expressed concern that more than any other group of pupils their "highly mobile students," defined as students who have moved three or more times before the fifth grade, are disengaged from their learning. . . . Teachers working with mobile students have the challenge of quickly integrating newcomers into established classrooms so instructional time is not lost and gaps in learning are kept to a minimum. (pp. 602–603)

To me it is a bit gut-wrenching to realize that some teachers are so fretful about losing "instructional time" that they can barely welcome a new child. I also find it alarming that a teacher might make a new child's "gaps in learning" the focus of initial interactions between the child and herself. But the fact is, those "gaps" will translate into low test scores on state-mandated standardized tests, for which the teacher's feet are being held to the fire. Besides, there are objectives to be met, and that leaves little time for teachers to actually engage children in meaningful conversations. Pinar (2009) writes, "Matching outcomes to objectives ensures that educational experience is replaced with institutional control by measurement" (p. 42). That is exactly what is going on with No Child Left Behind—*control by measurement*. It is difficult to be the caring, intuitive teacher when one's strings are being tightly pulled from above. But, as Lash and Kirkpatrick (1990) note, "In the absence of school programs, the major responsibility for working with children who move rests with the classroom teacher" (p. 178). Perhaps if the anvil of No Child Left Behind is lifted off the shoulders of educators, a creative teacher might be able to make a newcomer feel valued, resulting in the child's own experiences and histories becoming a welcome addition to the classroom community. For now, the usual routine is that the new kid is introduced, told where to sit, and then expected to blend in and catch up.

I am in a unique position when it comes to discussing the pertinent issues encased in the issue of student mobility. My own K-12 school list is long, and it spans the country; my life experience has provided for me a deeply personal understanding of the nomadic life of a child. And as a classroom teacher, I have also felt the frustrations that stemmed from having my class "vibe" change, knowing I was expected to quickly remediate a mid-year transfer child whenever necessary, and fearing that the student might pull down class averages on test scores. During those highly clueless couple of years in the beginning of my teaching career, I was no different from Ms. Baja, allowing my own panic about staying on track to guide my responses to children who "disrupted" the class with their arrival. However, my roots as a Geographic Cure Child finally trumped the frustrated teacher in me, and I found

CHAPTER 3

ways to connect with my transfer students. I was able to learn from them how I could help them adjust. Nevertheless, I do understand the cause *behind* the exasperated sigh that rises up from teachers when new students arrive on their doorsteps.

> Teachers wonder how to teach students who come and go. Nurses express frustration in delayed medical records due to frequent student movement. . . . Today, the increasing number of children and youth identified as homeless or highly mobile challenges schools in unique ways. (Milenkiewicz, 2005, p. i)

Many teachers who have issues with being given late transfer students are not mean-spirited people. They are caring, competent teachers who want to connect with their students. However, a big part of the problem is that they simply feel unprepared to handle the tasks set before them when the new child arrives, and they don't have enough knowledge of the circumstances surrounding mobility to realize how traumatic it is for the student. Teachers have just not been given time to think through ways in which they could help make the transition to the new class go more smoothly. A responsive teacher might also reflect upon the question of whether or not preconceived notions about transiency might influence the manner in which she approaches "the new kid," especially if she has been told in advance about a list of past schools.

In a report about generally held low expectations of urban students' learning potential, Flanigan (2005) lists "transient students" as one of the markers used to indicate probable low academic achievement (p. 41). Reporting on the efforts of a Grand Rapids school to counteract these low expectations, Flanigan points out that the school being studied is in one of the poorest neighborhoods of the city, and that "Teachers were frustrated by an increasing number of transient students—it is not uncommon for about half of the students in a given classroom to leave during a school year" (pp. 40–41). Frustration contributes to feelings of powerlessness and lack of control of the situation.

Then there are teachers who feel put-upon to deal with transiency. The new teacher who is drowning in paperwork and discipline problems says she cannot handle one more challenge. The veteran teacher thinks the child should be sent across the hall, or next door, or anywhere besides her room, because her children are "all involved in projects" that the new child will know nothing about. When these negative vibes hit a new child square in the face, the stage is set for another miserable school experience. Teachers in these cases have forgotten that it's *not* all about them. They make little or no effort to grasp what's going on for the new child in their charge. As Franke et al. (2003) write:

> The extent to which families move in urban settings cannot be ignored as a cause for the difficulties of school-age children. School transience has been found to be detrimental to academic achievement and may also have effects on self-esteem and classroom behavior, as well as on the *perceptions held by educators* regarding academic ability and motivation. (p. 150) (emphasis added)

Children who move often are often heartbroken children. If, in their previous location, they made friends, had a few family members nearby, or established a trusting relationship with the last teacher they had, leaving that location for the next is unbearable. As Hango (2006) explains:

> Essentially, when families move, they break ties with significant others, and the result is the disruption of important relationships. . . . Moreover, these relationships often served as effective sanctions for monitoring and guiding positive behavior, such as good study habits. Thus, the loss of important community relationships through mobility often results in a decrease in educational attainment. (p. 633)

If, however, in that prior location, the children were miserable and had no friends, the prospect of moving yet again may convince them that misery is just par for the course of their lives. In either case, such kids are beaten down, and school achievement is not their primary concern. And their teachers are at a loss as to how to help them.

Some teachers, upon finding no speedy remedy for problems they face, will abandon the effort rather than dig deeper. Britzman and Pitt (1996) noted a tendency in student teachers to give up quickly:

> We notice how difficult it is for student teachers to work through their doubt and anxiety, to engage creatively with the uncertainties of their own learning, and to stay within a difficult problem without recourse to finding quick solutions or to give up when problems seem too big. . . . These responses are, in a sense, provoked by the structure of teacher education and the epistemology of education itself, with its push toward remedy, control and expertise. (p. 119)

The reactions of the student teachers who sought quick solutions, choosing not to stay with a problem long enough to work through it, mirror the search for the Geographic Cure. My assertion is that before even beginning their careers, those student teachers seemed to already sense the pressure from above to find a quick fix and meet policy makers' expectations, come hell or high water. Possibly they felt unease about becoming the next wave of teachers expected to raise test scores.

The academic achievement of highly mobile children is fast becoming a chief concern of the teachers and principals whose schools will be affected by the students' "academic performance." The pressure on schools from the district level upward throws teachers into dread mode each time another new child arrives. Responsive teaching, which takes into account each individual student's background, experiences, talents, and interests, as well as intelligence, can barely be accomplished under existing constraints with children who report to school at the beginning of the year. When a new student arrives months after the opening of school, responsive teaching may not be at the top of anyone's agenda. As Pinar (2009) contends, "Instead of educational opportunities offered," teaching has indeed become "a contract promising to produce 'results,' that is, rising test scores" (p. 11).

CHAPTER 3

Even when the children arrive too close to a state-mandated test to "count against" the school's scores (for which they are all immensely grateful), there is still another test around the bend. School administrators and teachers don't like being responsible for children who have drifted in and out of multiple schools. Franke et al. (2003) address the problem of accountability in regard to mobility:

> Support systems for children and families, who are often mobile, need to be built into the school's infrastructure and incorporated into its culture. This may be particularly true given the current focus on results-based accountability and its emphasis on testing. Mobility in urban schools is such a pervasive issue affecting such large numbers of students that no special program with limited capacity or short duration can address the issue sufficiently. Urban schools must acknowledge this new reality and build an infrastructure that supports success for these children. (p. 150)

Striving to meet measurable goals and have children "perform," hoping fervently not to be placed on the state's "Needs Improvement" list, schools are in reality leaving countless children *behind*. In my mind, highly mobile children are among the groups most adversely affected by the current accountability rage. Darling-Hammond (1998) writes, "We are entering an era in which all people must learn flexibly and effectively to survive and succeed in this fast-changing world (p. 78). However, many teachers struggle to simply survive in the insanely (erratically) fast-changing world of education; they are frazzled and frustrated. It stands to reason, then, that the children who drop into their classrooms mid-year or even later stand little chance of surviving as well.

Beyond military and migrant situations, there are hundreds of other circumstances prompting frequent moves that have the potential to make life exceedingly difficult for children. Complicating the issue further is the fact that "moving on" has become the norm in modern culture. Bauman (2012) explains that "passages from the 'solid' to a 'liquid' phase of modernity . . . can no longer (and are not expected to) keep their shape for long, because they decompose and melt faster than the time it takes to cast them" (p. 1). The quick-paced, global citizen of today is fine with moving on quickly to greener pastures. Yet, Bauman also adds, "It is around places that human experience tends to be formed and gleaned, that life-sharing is attempted to be managed, and life meanings are conceived, absorbed, and negotiated" (p. 81). A school-aged child who is continually on the move finds that life meanings conceived are quickly thrown over for the next set; there is little time for them to be absorbed, not to mention negotiated.

The ways in which frequent family moves impact children emotionally are deep and varied, yet the support base for school-aged children on the move is wildly inconsistent. As I see it, the collision of student mobility with teacher/school accountability is universal regardless of the particular set of family issues. My contention is that pressure from standardization and Adequate Yearly Progress keeps school personnel from helping children on the move find ways to cope with their paper-thin stability. Bainbridge (2003) asserts, "There would appear to be no higher priority than finding ways to help families and social-service agencies understand that moving students from place to place hinders their educational progress" (p. 2). I would certainly expand on Bainbridge's assertion to include educators as well. I've seen much cluelessness in the classroom regarding the stressors endured by frequently mobile students. Worse, I've seen such children (especially mid-year placements or later) resented and complained about openly, instead of genuinely welcomed and valued. When there's a case of *teachers behaving badly*, it has been my observation that the root cause is nearly always panic mode, pure and simple: "What will this kid do to my scores?" What a travesty for both student and teacher, to be put in such a position.

CHAPTER 4

DRINKING AND DRIVING (AWAY)

INSET: GEOGRAPHY AND HIS SISTER

When we moved to Los Angeles from Washington, D.C. at the end of my second-grade year, I thought we would see glamorous movie stars on every corner, palm trees reaching to the sky, fancy cars, and fancier restaurants. I also expected to be near my Aunt Mamie, my mother's sister, since *that was the whole point* of moving to California to begin with. What I saw instead were old high-rise apartment buildings, lots of concrete, and a small market. Our apartment was on the sixth floor of one of shabbier buildings in the area. The only palm tree in sight was a solitary one that had seen better days; it didn't seem to care whether it reached to the sky or not.

As things turned out, we lived nowhere near Aunt Mamie. Her home was a nice spread on the side of a hill, miles away. Mamie found our "suitable" living arrangement for us before we arrived, but in my state of poutiness, I felt like the only person whom the choice *suited* was Mamie. We certainly needed to be able to afford the rent, but it seemed to me we could have found something closer. I was hurt that Aunt Mamie was far away. On our way out to Los Angeles my mother had been talking up a storm about how great it would be to be near *family.* We'll get together as a *family.* No one is more important than *family.* I was an only child at that point, and my family had just crumbled: my parents divorced for the second time, and my dad was a "zillion miles away" back east.

Marcia discovered that she was pregnant soon after my parents' divorce papers were signed. She delayed telling my father until we were ready to leave Washington. He had been pleading with her not to take me so far away, but Marcia was convinced that she needed to make the move. She had been drinking heavily, but planned to stop; this new beginning would be just the ticket. Had my dad known that there was a baby on the way, he would have pressured her even more to stay. But he had no idea. They barely saw each other, and she hid her shape successfully until we were leaving for good. Marcia basically tossed the news over her shoulder to my dad as we were boarding the plane. If Marcia had any qualms about being a pregnant, single mother, she must have shaken them off. Her only focus was to get to Los Angeles to be near her sister. This determination is quite curious as I look back now: the two sisters fought like rabid raccoons their entire lives. As an eight-year-old, I had no idea of their family history, but I sure saw the claws come out once we had been there a few days. Mamie was older, and had what Marcia considered a

CHAPTER 4

condescending, "bossy" air about her. My aunt and their older brothers had all left home by the time my mother was in junior high, but they all had "one foot out the door" even earlier than that. (Marcia often referred to herself as a "change-of-life baby," but I had no idea what that meant.) My mother wasn't about to let her older sister boss her around.

The pregnancy was an excellent reason for my mother not to work, so we lived on child support from my dad. We rarely went out unless Aunt Mamie came to get us for dinner (we had no car at that time). Mamie nagged Marcia about drinking while pregnant, so my mother finally declined all future invitations. I was exceedingly miserable in that apartment and could not wait for school to start. I thought maybe I'd finally make a friend. When the school year began, I came home that first day with three brand new textbooks: math, reading, and a subject I had never heard of before then—*geography*. I loved how shiny and clean the new books were, and especially loved the new subject. I turned pages of that brand new textbook and looked at maps of countries and pictures of rivers, mountains, llamas, and brightly colored clothing. *Neat!*

The school year had only just begun when my mother went into labor. Mamie came to take us to the hospital, and a baby boy was delivered by Caesarean section. When it was time for the baby to come home, I was thrilled. He was the most beautiful baby to have ever been born. My aunt and mother were hesitant to let me hold my new brother, but the minute I had my hands on him, I fell in love. *I have a brother. A baby brother! I am his sister. I'm a big sister! There are two of us now!* There was no jealousy. Just pure, overwhelming delight.

My mother left some papers from the hospital on the table, including my brother's birth certificate. I looked at that paper and was horrified. *She has named my brother "Geography." Geography! How stupid!* I stared at the word, realizing that it didn't look quite right. Aunt Mamie saw the look on my face, and explained: "This is the British spelling for the name 'Jeffrey.'" *OH! Geoffrey! Oh, thank goodness.* My aunt said the name had to do with our Scottish heritage. I couldn't see how the letters "geo" could sound like "jef," but that didn't matter. I had a brother, he was *not* named after a textbook, and all was right with the world. What a poetic little mistake, considering how our lives continued to be led.

I loved my father deeply, but I was very mad at him for not staying married to my mother. We were not a family anymore. Then Aunt Mamie turned out to prefer keeping her distance from my mother, which meant from me as well. But this little baby brother made me feel so much love that I thought my heart would pop out of my chest. In my ignorance, I believed that I finally understood the term "change-of-life baby." *Geoffrey changed my life.* I had "family" regardless of what all the *stupid adults* in my life were doing. As soon as I realized that I could make that baby smile, I was done for. And as soon as I realized that my mother would not be able to care for Geoffrey without help (despite the fact that she loved him to pieces) I found an assertiveness within myself that had never surfaced before. My brother. My family. "I'll take him," I told my mother. "You go sit down."

GLASS CASTLES AND GEOGRAPHY LESSONS

> We might enroll in school, but not always. Mom and Dad did most of our teaching. Mom had us reading books without pictures by the time we were five, and Dad taught us math. He also taught us things that were really important and useful, like how to tap out Morse code and how we should never eat the liver of a polar bear because all the vitamin A in it could kill us.
>
> —Jeanette Walls, *The Glass Castle*

When Children of Alcoholics paddle down the river of booze that is "home," nights are especially scary. Dark is the enemy, because the drunk parent loves the dark. Often, the blue glow from the television is the only source of light. The parent lets loose at night, even if he/she has to go to work in the morning. At night, yelling and screaming *feel* louder, more threatening. Nights are chaotic and frightening. "Bed time" is an abstract concept at best.

Children of Alcoholics go to school sleep-deprived, ill, and anxious on the mornings that follow a parent's "bad night." They will worry about whether or not the parent made it to work. They worry about what awaits them at home that evening. They worry. However, for Geographic Cure Children living the Life Erratic, that river is even more treacherous. A torrential current pulls these children under, and then pitches them back out at the door of *yet another* new place to live, and *yet another* new school. The devastating combination of parental alcoholism *and* frequent family mobility is the nucleus of this book—my battleground, as Marla Morris (2009) puts it. As I indicated in Chapter 2, Alcoholics Anonymous (n.d.) uses the term "Geographic Cure" to describe the problem drinker who moves on to the next location, in hopes that a new beginning is all that's needed, *then* he or she will stop drinking. It is my contention that children living the Life Erratic are transient children whose frequent school changes are directly tied to the alcoholic parent's unending quest for that Geographic Cure. I was a Geographic Cure Child during my school-age years, and I use my story to illustrate the Life Erratic. More importantly, I've taught many Geographic Cure Children, and I've worked with teachers who have taught them. I know how easy it is for them to slip under the radar. Their school records give only the "highly mobile" picture. I am telling the rest of the story. I bring them front and center into the spotlight of education as it is today, when accountability pressures have many classroom teachers buckling at the knees. As discussed in Chapter 3, there are teachers who balk upon seeing a new student entering their classrooms. The countenance of such teachers does not always mask their concern (and sometimes resentment) that the child will disturb the class equilibrium, not to mention the class standardized test report. This unwelcoming perception of the child then remains with the teachers for the duration of the child's stay. I hope that by contributing to an understanding of the Life Erratic, I am opening a door for teachers to consider carefully and discuss provocatively the difficulties of this life for the Geographic Cure Child in their midst. With this book, I hope to start a dialogue that continues for quite some time.

CHAPTER 4

In Chapter 2, I mentioned two authors whose memoirs speak directly to the lived experiences of Geographic Cure Children. Both memoirs are spellbinding, and both, in my opinion, should be required reading for all educators in schools, as well as in the academy. Jeannette Walls, author of *The Glass Castle*, is a journalist and writer who grew up with her siblings in a family situation that precisely typifies the experience of Geographic Cure Children. Walls lived in the "and"—she was a Child of an Alcoholic *and* a transient child. Walls' parents preferred to live a roving existence, moving from one place to another in the southwest United States and in the mountains. When the family ran out of money, her alcoholic father Rex stepped up these cure-seeking moves from place to place, skipping out on rent, and running from trouble, wife and children in tow. Rex drank like a fiend and would disappear for days. Since their mother had stability issues of her own, and since the family's quality of life deteriorated more at every turn, Walls and her siblings had to fend for themselves. They also had to "parent" their parents.

The Walls' frequent moves meant that the children spent large amounts of time out of school. This did not mean, however, that the children were not learning. For example, Walls (2005), who was a voracious reader, recalls:

> I loved *The Grapes of Wrath*, *Lord of the Flies*, and especially *A Tree Grows in Brooklyn*. I thought Francie Nolan and I were practically identical, except that she had lived fifty years earlier in Brooklyn and her mother always kept the house clean. Francie Nolan's father sure reminded me of Dad. If Francie saw the good in her father, even though most people considered him a shiftless drunk, maybe I wasn't a complete fool for believing in mine. Or trying to believe in him. It was getting harder. (pp. 168–169)

Walls, her brother, and sisters simply had a different skill set than children who sat in classrooms all day long. This fact underscores my conviction that no one should presume that Geographic Cure Children are not *knowledgeable* or *responsible*. The children are a wealth of knowledge, experience, and adaptability, and, in fact, have *much to contribute* to the school community. In a *New York Times* book review of *The Glass Castle*, critic Francine Prose (2005) noted, "Surely it suggests something about our educational system that whenever the Walls children did attend school they turned out to be academically ahead of the local kids, who tormented them for their outsider oddness." This one memoir provides a deep and profound understanding of the Life Erratic for Geographic Cure Children. When Walls' book first came out, her stories of sporadic schooling, and of her *actual* education that blossomed from lived experience, increased public awareness of such a life by leaps and bounds. I gave the book to coworkers and friends, saying, "*This* is what I've been talking about!"

The second memoir of a Geographic Cure Child that I find indispensable comes from Professor Michael Keith, who teaches communication at Boston College. His memoirs recall a significant part of his childhood that was spent on the road (literally) with his alcoholic father, and his stories are disquieting. He writes of hitchhiking with his father in sizzling heat, eating only sporadically, dragging his father out of bars, and missing school for months at a time. How very pertinent to my book that Keith's memoir is titled, *The Next Better Place*. Keith (2004) writes:

> The insatiable urge to leave, to take off for better places—places my father and I imbue with illusory mystery and magic—governs and rules us. It's a beggar's banquet of seedy homeless shelters, dreary rooming houses, church rectories, AA meetings, bus depots, oddball characters, endless highways, and hardships mitigated by the irresistible allure and promise of the next destination. The road map is our bible. (p. 285)

Keith's memoir has an adventurous tone because he wrote from the viewpoint of his early-adolescent self, who was happy to miss school, and who desperately wanted to trust his father that indeed, the next place would be far better. The truthful portrait he paints of his nomadic life gives the reader significant insight into the Geographic Cure, in its most literal sense, from his child's-eye view. Keith did clarify in his epilogue that as he grew into adulthood, he was livid with his father for dragging a starving young boy across the country on an alcohol-driven quest. It took Keith decades to get past the anger. However, as they traveled across the United States from New York to California, the young boy tried to maintain faith in his father's promises that in California, life would be better. Despite the omnipresent neglect he experienced, Keith acquired skills during that time that have remained with him for life. There are enlightening accounts in the book of how the child learned to quickly adapt to his current situation and relate to the people he came across. He visited local libraries to read as much as possible, and to learn about each city and state that they passed through. Keeping a map, he learned about geography by living on the road, rather than from a textbook (Keith, 2004).

As I described in previous chapters, my brother Geoff and I also lived through some harrowing experiences as Geographic Cure Children, including one particular episode that I now see in my mind's eye as a poster for the term. The picture shows my mother, plastered, collapsed against the passenger window of a "raggedy" old car. Beside her, in the driver's seat (in more ways than one) is 15-year-old me, driving our family from Merritt Island, Florida to Atlanta, Georgia. I am hunched forward, squinting, trying to ascertain if I'm steering the car in the right direction. My seven-year-old brother sits on the very edge of the back seat, leaning up toward the front seat, so that I can hear him. (My window and the back windows are down, because the car's air conditioning system is broken.) Geoff is holding in his hands a road map from the gas station, tracing the lines on the map with his finger to confirm that yes, we're headed toward Atlanta. We are hopeful that we are truly going the right direction, *this time*. We three passengers in that old, beat-up wagon were living the metaphor of the Geographic Cure.

For as far back as I can remember, I lived with a mother who was miserable no matter where she lived. "Identity forms emerge in the interaction between space and place" (Helfenbein, 2006, p. 92), but Marcia's identity was as blurred as her vision. She lived between the space of misery and some elusive better place she saw for

CHAPTER 4

herself, a magical dwelling place out there somewhere, where she would finally settle and get her act together. Marcia dragged us into that in-between, and Geoff and I could only barely form a sense of who we were. This was especially true for me before my brother came into my world. I was always an outsider. When I was very young, we did not live in any one place long enough for me to feel like I belonged.

My father, a young, injured World War II veteran, went to the University of the South in Sewanee, Tennessee, after his discharge. While at Sewanee, he met my mother, who grew up in nearby Chattanooga. They married, then moved to Dallas, Texas, where my dad taught Latin to eighth-grade boys in a private boys' school. I was born there in Dallas. Six months after I was born, Marcia decided that she hated that city, so they moved to Nashville. Then she decided she hated my father, divorced him, won custody of me, and took me to Huntsville, Alabama. My father moved to Washington, D.C. but "sent" for me as often as possible. (I was riding buses and flying on airplanes between parents, traveling alone, from the time I was four years old. There were no unaccompanied minor procedures back then. One parent saw me off; the other was waiting when I arrived.) While in Huntsville, my mother changed rooming houses and apartments within the city three times. I went to two different schools for kindergarten, and then another new school for first grade. There were six changes in personnel for my after-school babysitter. (They always quit. She wouldn't come home on time.) My mother decided that she loved my dad after all, so we moved to Washington, D.C., and my parents remarried.

My dad tried very hard to stay married to Marcia that second time, just as he had the first time around. We lived in Washington long enough that I stayed in one school for all of second grade. However, Marcia's drinking put my dad over the edge; he could not remain married to her, despite his love for me. They divorced, and he lost the second custody battle as well (judges in the 1960s thought children needed their mothers, period). My dad begged Marcia to remain in Washington, but she decided that it was time to get the hell out of Dodge. She was certain that she would stop drinking if she could move to California and live near her sister. Reluctantly, my dad bought our tickets, not knowing then that Marcia was pregnant with my brother. A few months later, Geoff was born in Los Angeles, where I spent *most* of third grade. However, we soon were back in Huntsville, where I was the "new girl" for the last two months of third grade. I had not yet turned nine years old, but was already well versed in being a stranger. I was the weirdo who kept her nose in a book at recess. It seems to me now that I was like the "Foreigner" whom Derrida (2000) describes:

> In truth, with the question he is getting ready to put, on the being of non-being, the Foreigner fears that he will be treated as mad (*manikos*). He is afraid of being taken for a son-foreigner-madman: "I am therefore fearful that what I have said may give you the opportunity of looking on me as someone deranged," says the translation. (p. 9)

Any time that I did begin to feel like an accepted citizen in my little classroom countries, I was whisked away, only to start again. There were times when I didn't even get to go back and retrieve belongings from my "cubby." When my mother was *in a mood*, arguing was futile. Better to keep things on an even keel. Better to be the buffer for my new brother.

Once we left Los Angeles, Marcia kept us in Huntsville for a little over two years. However, when it was time for me to begin fourth grade, I did not return to the school where I ended third grade. We apartment-hopped all over the city during those two years, which meant changing schools. I attended two schools for fourth grade, then one for fifth grade and half of sixth grade. While I was in the middle of that sixth-grade year, my mother decided to marry a man and take on his three children. She figured she would stop drinking if she could be part of a happy, blended family. Therefore, the rest of my sixth grade year was spent in Cocoa Beach, Florida, where we moved after the wedding. I would not spend seventh grade there, however. From Cocoa Beach we moved to Merritt Island.

A departure from my life's norm occurred at this point. I actually was able to attend the same school for all of junior high, which included seventh, eighth, and ninth grades. Plus, I managed to attend the local high school for one year, before being uprooted again. During that time period we also lived in our first nice house, in a lovely neighborhood. What went on *inside* that house, however, was a *fresh hell* of another story (two alcoholic parents, double the screaming, laced with horrendous physical abuse of Marcia). My last two years of high school were subsequently spent in Atlanta, Georgia. Such is the journey of a Geographic Cure Child.

THE BUFFER HAS NO BUFFER

When I use the term "Geographic Cure Children," I have in mind for the most part the Children of Alcoholics who are being hauled around from pillar to post by a single parent, as was my case for all but those four *blended family* years. Frequent mobility occurs more often in a single-parent household (U.S. Census Bureau, 2011). Having only one parent who is frequently a *drunk* parent makes coping with the alcoholism acutely problematic for the child. Discussing parental alcoholism in general, Werner and Johnson (2004) state that "the more supportive the non-alcoholic parent, the more likely there is available the nurturance, protection, and guidance that children need for optimal development" (p. 707). However, what happens if there is no other parent? What if the second parent is an enabler? Worse, what if the second one is also an alcoholic, as was the case when my mother was married those four years to my stepfather, a man who could drink her under the table?

Some researchers studying the impact of parental alcoholism suggest that a supportive second family member is likely to offset some of the distress of Children of Alcoholics (Bennet, Wolin, & Reiss, 1998). In my case, there was no such luxury. In Jeanette Walls' case, the second parent only contributed to the problem. In Michael Keith's case, the second parent gave him up. So there we were, and there, too, are many Geographic Cure Children right now: in a parent/child relationship resulting "in an unstable attachment style, inconsistent care, and inferior responses

CHAPTER 4

to children's needs" (Lussier, Laventure, & Bertrand, 2010, p. 1574), with the additional trauma of moving every time the wind changes.

Whenever we relocated, Marcia enrolled me in school. I did not have the experience of long periods of time away from the classroom, as did Walls and Keith. Instead, I was expected to get myself to and from school, and once back home, remain there alone with my baby brother until past my bedtime. I was a "latchkey" child—an underage child who has no one at home to care for them before and after school. Geoff's babysitter arrived when I left for the bus stop, but stayed only until I came in from school in the afternoons. My mother did not want to pay for any additional time. Robinson and Rhoden (1989) note that today there is great emphasis on latchkey children in general: society has created for them before- and after-school day care, neighborhood safety net adults, training sessions on personal safety, and so on. However, I was afforded none of those opportunities back in the early 1960s.

Sometimes, when my mother applied the Geographic Cure to her job situation as well, she would be home during the day. In those instances, there was no babysitter. Such times were *never* an improvement. Having an alcoholic at home who has been drinking all day is no picnic. I much preferred to return from school to "take over" and wave goodbye to the babysitter. When Marcia was home, she would be very territorial about my brother's care. Routines that I had established were eschewed because after all, *she* was the mother. *I* was the child. She would be venomous, and I would have to walk on eggshells even more than usual. If I was careful, I could keep peace in the household by simply waiting. Soon, Marcia would fall asleep (while the Dinty Moore Stew can sat in the kitchen opened, but unheated). Then I could take care of my brother and myself. Unfortunately, many Children of Alcoholics are not officially classified as latchkey children (and not on their school's radar) if the parent is technically home. "Many kids who go home each day to an alcoholic parent do not get the adequate preparation they need for self-care. . . . The parent may be so physically and psychologically unavailable that the child is literally unsupervised" (Robinson & Rhoden, 1998, p. 93). And then there is the child who goes home alone, ostensibly for a relatively short time, while the parent "winds up the work day." In my case, the parent preferred to *wind down* at Happy Hour before coming home.

I now add to this puzzle another piece: the high-mobility factor. Children of Alcoholics whose parents do not relocate frequently have more possibilities for support, from *somewhere*. Geographic Cure Children do not. The bottom line is that they are forever moving on. Walls (2005) writes, "We were always doing the skedaddle, usually in the middle of the night" (p. 19). Although for Children of Alcoholics, keeping the family secrets safely hidden is paramount, there may nevertheless be a neighbor or relative in whom they might confide—an informed supporter. For that matter, just knowing the *names* of neighbors, being able to recognize them and know that they recognize the child, can make the child feel safer if an emergency arises. When children attend schools regularly and over a span of some years, those children are *known* to the school. Even if the child thinks he or she is keeping the secrets of parental drinking safe, there may be covert support mechanisms in place, or, at the very least, an awareness. For the Geographic Cure Child, such threads of support, however thin they may be, are unavailable. Those threads are not *known* to the child. This is the crux of the matter: Geographic Cure Children are on their own in the most profound sense. Physically, emotionally, in the midst of community, on their own.

ON THE FINE ART OF CIGARETTE REMOVAL

Returning for a moment to parentification (role reversal) as described in Chapter 2, I stress that in relationships between alcoholics and their children, the child is often "called upon to play the role of the adult, a role that does not correspond to the child's developmental level" (Lussier et al., 2010, p. 1574). Roles are vital to the survival plan of a Child of an Alcoholic. They are, as Devine and Braithwaite (1993) note, "coping responses of children who are threatened by their family situation" (p. 76). This role reversal is a more difficult burden to bear for a Geographic Cure Child who has no one *but* that alcoholic parent (whom they "parent") to depend upon.

For example, as a young child I was terrified of fire, and was convinced each night that Marcia would burn the place down before dawn. She stayed up very late "watching TV" (read: drinking nonstop) with the rest of the lights off. She would eventually "fall asleep in front of the TV" (read: pass out). Rather than leave her in the living room, I used to pester my plonkered mother to wake up and come to bed, because that was the only way *I* could attempt sleep. We always shared a bedroom, and having twin beds meant that I was never more than four feet away when Marcia snored through the night. I hated that snoring, but if I could get her into bed, she wouldn't *smoke* in the bed. If I woke up and saw her still in bed, I could go back to sleep. In the living room, however, she would "fall asleep" with a cigarette between her fingers. I was always afraid that Marcia would unknowingly start a fire, not wake up, and burn us all to pieces. (A variation on this theme did come to fruition once, as recounted in the inset for Chapter 2.) However, once my mother was in the bed, I could relax somewhat, since for some inexplicable reason smoking in bed was never her thing. Marcia lost many security deposits because of cigarette burns on the living room carpets, but never the bedroom floor.

The black/brown charred spots were always in one little area, like wagons circled under the side of her chair where the ashtray was located. There were holes in the chairs themselves as well, and on the couches, of every one of Marcia's apartments, for her entire life, until she had to move to an assisted living facility. I can still smell the singed cheap upholstery stuffing today. This was quite an issue for our landlords, who were always angry and unyielding about deposits when we left. I attempted to save the carpets or flooring as much as possible. Those attempts were only partially about protecting Marcia's deposits, however. I was much more concerned with protecting us all from fire, and protecting Geoff and myself from the guaranteed "bender" that would ensue when we moved from a place without the deposit. (Children of Alcoholics always try to head off at the pass any extra reasons

CHAPTER 4

to drink that might be predicted and possibly dodged.) In each new apartment, I tried to keep the carpet or flooring free from burns, but it rarely worked out. Marcia was like *Lost Weekend's* Don Birnam (how poetic the name sounds, in this instance), whose fingers were covered in cigarette burns after a binge: "There were three or four small burns between the index- and middle-fingers of each hand where he had held cigarettes too long—always the surest sign that he had been drinking himself unconscious and for days" (Jackson, 1963, p. 246).

If I wanted to watch TV a while longer when Marcia "drifted off," I would turn some lights back on and then gingerly (*easy does it . . . careful . . .*) try to slide the still-lit cigarettes away from her fingers to put them out. This was an *art*. Cigarette removal was always very tricky business. (When Geoff was older, he mastered this art as well, and we'd watch television together while she drooled, wig cocked to one side, false teeth halfway out of her mouth. That was our sense of *peace in the home.*) If Marcia woke up and caught me, she would be furious to find me taking that cigarette away. She would insist that she was still "listening" to whatever show was on, smash the cigarette in the ashtray, light up another one, then stomp into the kitchen to get a "nightcap," all the while yelling at me to mind my own business. Since this usually happened late at night, I would try to shut the door to my baby brother's room, but Marcia interpreted this action as an editorial comment. Her indignant response would escalate the tension even more. Later at night, when I decided that I could probably get Marcia to go to bed, I would wake the sleeping dragon and announce, "It's late, let's go to bed—we have to get up in the morning." Amazingly, she would often allow me push/drag her back to her cave when I mentioned *morning*, as long as I wasn't touching her cigarette. She would even put the thing out herself.

Who can sleep with unwatched cigarettes burning in the living room in the middle of the night? Who can be alert for the math test the following day? Who can tell a "trusted adult" what's going on when there is *no* trusted adult in the tri-state area, because no adult is known? Who at school would notice that a child is sleep-deprived, when no one knows the child at all? Morehouse and Richards (1986) note that basic human needs such as food and shelter include, for a child, consistency in "where the child sleeps, with whom he sleeps, and when he sleeps," (p. 93). Yet, in one typical clinical case of a Child of an Alcoholic, an eight-year-old boy (who was being treated for hyperactivity) lived in constant upheaval regarding what time, where, and with whom he would sleep:

> If father was "too drunk," mother came into the child's room and ousted him from his bed, and the boy was sent to another of his sibling's rooms to sleep in either a top bunk bed alone, a double bed with his sister, or a single bed with another brother. (Morehouse & Richards, 1986, p. 93)

Imagine being admonished, or worse, humiliated for falling asleep in class. Now imagine being the "new kid," who doesn't have friends in the class with whom you can *laugh it off* later. Instead, you are the crazy, disgraced Foreigner who is *laughed at*, and scolded for disrupting the lesson. And then, to top it all off, you are rebuked for not caring about school. "When will you ever learn to be responsible?" the teacher asks. She is aggravated, and more than likely she is simply unaware that you are typical of the many Children of Alcoholics who display poor academic performance (Marcus, 1986). That same night, you again feed your baby brother, bathe him, read to him, sing to him, and put him to sleep. Later you march the dragon back to the cave. Before you know it, you're the new student again in a different classroom. In The Next Better Home, there are new holes for the dragon to burn. You get better and better at not disturbing your borderline mother—you lay low, and try not to be "fooled by the eye of the storm" (Lawson, 2004, p. 27). You distance yourself.

Mylant, Ide, Cuevas, and Meehan (2002) define children's "adaptive distancing" as "healthy detachment from their parents' chemical dependency problem," and assert that "detaching, yet remaining aware and concerned, can become the most important form of self-care for these children" (p. 63). Children of Alcoholics can greatly benefit from resources "such as Alateen, school nurses, and counselors. School nurses are often the first to identify a Child of an Alcoholic because of the increased tendency toward physical complaints" (Mylant et al., 2002, p. 63). What is tragic is that Geographic Cure Children who move fluidly in and out of schools don't always learn about these resources. They "missed that day." So they rely upon themselves to figure things out. They miss much, indeed.

As I mentioned in Chapter 2, in my own case, especially when my brother was old enough to share private jokes with me, my most effective coping mechanism was the use of humor. I tried to find ways to *make fun of it*—whatever the "it" of the day turned out to be. As an Adult Child of an Alcoholic, I do so still. Actress Carrie Fischer (of *Star Wars* fame) writes with wry humor in her autobiography, *Wishful Drinking* (2008), about her dysfunctional Hollywood upbringing and her own substance-abusing life. Her honesty and wit appeal to me because she approaches her traumatic life with a glorious, smart-ass attitude. I can appreciate Fischer's use of humor as a primary defense mechanism. As far as I'm concerned, Fischer is in The Club—mine and my brother's, along with some friends, a few co-workers, and even an occasional professor. *Make fun of it.* Fischer (2008) explains that she was "a clumsy-looking and intensely awkward, insecure little girl" who "decided then that I'd better develop something else—if I wasn't going to be pretty, maybe I could be funny or smart—someone past caring. So far past caring that you couldn't even see it with a telescope" (p. 50). Therefore, she developed her amazing wit, which served her well, even when, in her adult life, she had to get sober.

As also discussed in Chapter 2, humor comes into play when the child is trying to keep the unhappy parent in a good mood. Inconsistency in the drunk parent's mood makes being funny dangerous work, however. What's amusing one day earns a slap the next day. However, the child keeps trying to be funny, despite the inconsistent responses, because *maybe* the parent will laugh, and a happy drunk parent is far preferable to an angry one. Carol Burnett (2003), who had *two* alcoholic parents, writes about the mercurial, unpredictable moods of her drunken parents, describing how she walked on eggshells while working twice as hard to be funny. In the classroom, some children who use humor as a coping strategy learn quickly how to stay on the safe side of sarcasm, but others stretch the limits too far, and have to learn the hard way how to scale things back a notch. Children who get to know their teachers learn how far they can go with "being funny." A new student, however, has to figure this out much more quickly, and that learning curve can be painful. Such is the quandary of the Geographic Cure Child.

SECRETS AND LIES, GOOD MOODS AND GOODBYES

Although Geographic Cure Children cope with all of the usual suspects in the line-up of traumas experienced (emotional problems, physical ailments, sleep issues, unpredictability, parentification, and more), I contend that what makes them distinct from others is the weight of bearing secrets *while in flight,* and the loneliness that comes from being *unknown* to their surroundings. Certainly, secrecy is a major stressor for most Children of Alcoholics. There is an added dimension of difficulty when one has to shoulder the 150-pound padlock that keeps the door to those secrets firmly closed, while being dragged by the hand from state to state, town to town, or simply neighborhood to neighborhood. There is a much slimmer chance of being noticed as a child who needs help because, as the new kid, disclosure is especially dangerous, as far as reprisal goes. Disclosure is just not going to happen. As Arman (2000) notes, "the denial, secrecy, and isolation present in alcoholic families often keeps children from being identified and helped" (p. 290).

Secrecy and isolation are magnified 100 times over for Geographic Cure Children, whose neighborhoods change like television channels on a Friday night. Black (1979) describes a child who would routinely "sit outside a bar in the car, waiting while his father drank for hours" (p. 24). Keith (2004) did the same thing with his father as they hitchhiked across the country, except that he wouldn't wait outside for long; he went inside the bars to drag his father out. How traumatic for a child to hang around a bar, waiting for a parent, in familiar surroundings. How terrifying doing so *in a different city* on a routine basis. How deep is the loneliness when there is no one on earth with whom to talk about these crises? Since frequent moves become par for the course for Geographic Cure Children, they make few friends, and in some places, *no* friends. Often, in a self-protective vein, frequently mobile children won't bother to make friends anyway, because they know they're on the way out as soon as they make their way in.

Some Geographic Cure Children spend much of their early life without meaningful, sustaining relationships in any context—family, neighborhood, or school. Schools are the places most likely to provide light for these children, since children spend more waking hours in the classroom than anywhere else, during the school year. In my own (long!) list of schools, I encountered more than a few teachers who made it clear to me that I was not welcome. As discussed in Chapter 3, there are educators in schools today who are defeated by the presence of a new student, thought to disrupt the status quo of the class. Perhaps this negative reaction does not stem from a mean-spirited source. I believe that a teacher's unwelcoming manner is likely a product of exasperation (with how little time they have to foster meaning*ful* pedagogical relationships with their students), and exhaustion (with the meaning*less* requirements being piled on them by "the higher-ups"). Of course, the child standing there in front of a class, feeling the sting of a teacher's "Oh, great. Thanks a lot!" unwelcome demeanor, has no idea why there is ill will in the air. He or she just knows that it's a familiar, sad feeling.

The dynamic between "new" teacher and "new" child becomes a power struggle between the Foreigner and the host country; to again use Derrida's (2000) description, "The Foreigner shakes up the threatening dogmatism of the paternal *logos:* the being that is, and the non being that is not. As though the Foreigner had to begin by contesting the authority of the chief" (p. 5). If the law of the classroom is the law of the authority of the Chief, then the student is the Foreigner who contests that authority by simply by daring to interrupt the status quo of the classroom community. The teacher may not perceive this interruption of the new student as a power struggle, because he or she is the "Chief," and the new student is a mere child. However, going back to my previous comment that the teacher may be exasperated by constraints and exhausted by demands, then it follows that the teacher may see the child as an interloper who is, in effect, telling him or her to *work harder.* And that "demand" will get many a teacher's hackles up. Price (2006) writes:

> In relation to individual pupils, it is easy for the teacher figure to become *all-powerful* and to incite rebellion. It is also easy for the teacher to avoid being held to account for their own part in this dynamic, their own projections onto pupils, as affected by the inevitable unconscious biases of their own inner relationships to authority. (p. 151)

The "new kid"/Foreigner may seem, to the teacher/Chief (however unconsciously), to be cut from the same cloth as the powers-that-be in schooling, who make countless unreasonable demands on him or her. However, the little Foreigner knows nothing of projections. The Geographic Cure child only knows that once again, he or she is the "new kid" who has no grasp of this new country he has been thrust into. The child has to learn new rules, new classroom "language," new procedures ("I don't know what you did in your other schools, but *this* is how we do things here . . ."). The teacher hopes the child will assimilate quickly. By entering the country of the classroom, this child is standing there, hat in hand, asking for hospitality, chagrined at having to do so in a strange place, *once again.* Derrida (2000) writes:

> He has to ask for hospitality in a language which by definition is not his own, the one imposed on him by the master of the house, the host, the king, the lord, the authorities, the nation, the State, the father, etc. This personage imposes on him translation into their own language, and that's the first act of violence. (p. 15)

Imagine the teacher's feelings upon learning that the child has not yet learned to "regroup" in math, or write a topic sentence in Language Arts. And for three nights in a row the child *has not bothered to do homework.* The Chief is not happy! The Geographic Cure Child has a single parent who won't come to the school for conferences. (From the child's point of view, if there is a God in Heaven, the parent never will come to the school. Having mom show up drunk at PTA is far worse than having mom not show up at all.) The little Foreigner is breaking all of the rules in the host country, but he or she never breaks the family rule about secrets. The child was forced to sign a (mental, emotional, spiritual) non-disclosure agreement long ago.

Who, then, can do *anything* for children who live the Life Erratic? Where do we start? Discerning, caring school counselors, nurses, and teachers are taught how to recognize signs of physical and emotional neglect. However, Children of Alcoholics, especially those who are transient, slip under the professionals' radar every day. Physical symptoms displayed by Children of Alcoholics are often rooted in emotional pain that is "manifested in physical symptomology"; therefore they may steadily complain "about stomachaches, headaches, and other physical ailments without explainable causes" (Lambie & Sias, 2005, p. 270). Within the medical community, these ailments are often inaccurately assessed, Lambie and Sias continue, "because both parents and children deny that they are living in a state of siege; therefore doctors have very few cues to lead them to look for alcohol abuse in their parents. Many physicians, however, join the denial brigade" (p. 22). Logic suggests that support avenues be made known to all children, hoping that the ones who need help will take advantage of the knowledge. *That* can be problematic. The need to talk with (hear about, read about) other children "in the same boat" is of paramount importance. There are in fact programs in some schools that do offer the chance for this to happen. However, participation in such programs requires parental permission for the child to attend. Ah, there's the rub! There is no way on this earth that I would have brought a note like that home. Cuijpers (2005) notes:

> (W)hen children do react to an active recruitment approach (or when they are identified by a screening instrument) a major ethical dilemma arises. Namely, it is not considered ethical to intervene with children without having a prior commitment and/or agreement from the parents. In this case, however, the parents themselves are the problem and, one assumes, they *will not easily allow* their child to participate in an intervention programme aimed at children of an identified problem drinker. (p. 468) (emphasis added)

"Will not easily allow . . ." what an understatement! My mother would have foamed at the mouth if I brought home from school some kind of permission form to attend a group for Children of Alcoholics. My need to talk with others who had experiences similar to mine conflicted mightily with Marcia's need for me to *shut the hell up.* Alcoholics who are not in a treatment program:

> are not likely to admit their alcoholism nor to encourage their children to seek treatment for conditions possibly related to the parents' drinking. Thus, gaining access to the COA population when the parent is not in treatment poses

a difficult problem for preventive interventions. (Roosa, Gensheimer, Short, Ayers, & Shell, 1989, p. 297)

What is encouraging is that a group of researchers brainstormed about ways to work *around* the disclosure/permission issue for Children of Alcoholics. As a result, schools in some states are now sending home forms that simply request parental permission for their children to participate "in groups to improve self-esteem and to learn about drug and alcohol prevention. This approach gets around stigmatizing anyone concerned" (Post & Robinson, 1998, pp. 5–6).

Alcohol abuse researchers Roosa et al. (1989) recommend to teachers in grades four through six that they show a film called "Lots of Kids Like Us," which depicts 10- to 12-year-old children "experiencing a number of crises" involving alcoholic parents, and then invite children who were interested in discussing the film to a *second* meeting later in the day (p. 297). Children who came to the second meeting were given permission forms to take home, which described the group as an extension of the school's substance abuse prevention program. The entire recruitment process, designed "to reduce children's reluctance to self-identify" garnered a response higher than expected: Close to two-thirds of those children came to the second meeting, and about one-third of that group sought parental permission to take part in the group (Roosa et al., 1989, pp. 297–298).

Another encouraging study found that teachers who felt ill-prepared to approach the subject of parental alcoholism with children still "were willing to explore the issue with students and correctly believed that COAs were unlikely to request help" (Knight et al., 1992, p. 370). I am gratified when teachers understand this; the point that Children of Alcoholics fear reprisal is huge. Some teachers don't want to broach the subject of parental alcoholism at all with children, preferring instead to leave such subjects to the school counselors. Yet the result of such a referral might mean sending a child out for "group" on a regular basis, and that doesn't work for all teachers. In my talks with many teachers whom I trained or mentored over the years, I heard time and again that as interested as they were in children's best interests, they could not imagine how time could be carved out of "the instructional day" for students to attend support groups, even if only twice a month. This is the accountability anvil, pressing down on their shoulders, doing the talking.

Additionally, when a new student is brought to the classroom, one of the first things a teacher will do is scramble to determine how much the child needs to "catch up" with the rest of the class. That brings the likelihood of allowing the child to leave the room for group sessions (or individual counseling) down to about zero, unless the child acts out, in which case leaving with the counselor is strongly encouraged! In most cases, the Child of an Alcoholic is not going to be disruptive in class, however. He or she is too skilled in keeping the peace to create a fuss.

Such is the Catch-22 of the Geographic Cure Child: The one who needs counseling most, due to frequent school changes, is likely not to receive it, due to frequent school changes. Either the problems at home are not known, or those problems cannot take

CHAPTER 4

precedent over standards, objectives, and test preparation. Years go by, Children of Alcoholics don't get help when they're young, and in no time they become teenagers who *still* haven't found positive ways to cope. Tinnfalt et al. (2011) found that many teenagers are open to support but need to be encouraged to trust the disclosure process:

> Adolescents want and need support from adults. They want social workers, teachers, school nurses, psychologists and other adults to be more sensitive in reading the signals that children and adolescents in a disclosure process send about problems at home. The signals can be more or less verbally explicit. Adults can ask more direct questions to get clarity about the home situation of children. However, the time may not be ready for the young person to be able to tell. It may come later in the revealing process. Adults need more education in how to support children and adolescents in the disclosure process, and the social authorities must send clear messages about their responsibilities and capabilities to support and help people in need. (p. 148)

WHISPERS IN THE ROAR

> Memoir is about handing over your life to someone and saying, this is what I went through, this is who I am, and maybe you can learn something from it.
> —Jeanette Walls, *The Glass Castle*

There are many Geographic Cure Children for whom Doll's (2006) description of "illuminating a silence" is so perfect:

> This idea of rupturing so as to illuminate a silence is highly provocative for educators, the root of education being to lead out that which lies within and of curriculum being to let course that which flows within. There is a world out there, or in there (p. 110).

One way in which the silences of Children of Alcoholics can be "heard" is through juvenile fiction. Throughout this book I've made references to literature that tells the story of a child's or adult's experience with alcoholism. I think there should be countless more, and I applaud juvenile fiction writers such as Jack Gantos, author of the *Joey Pigza* series, for tackling a complicated theme. Young students can read themselves *into* a support group of sorts, just by reading fiction that deals with their topic. Through dialogue (reader response) journals, kept at school, the child and teacher might have some "discussions" about the characters in these books without saying anything out loud or sending anything home.

> Young children might, for developmental reasons, not understand that their situation is not like that of every child. Children of all ages can repress or dissociate the problem. . . . Hence not all COA are conscious of the problem, others will be reluctant to tell, and some are identified as COA. (Tinnfalt et al., 2011, p. 134)

Fiction is a way for Children of Alcoholics to see that they are not alone (by far!). As an educator as well as an Adult Geographic Cure Child, I am particularly drawn to the idea of seeking out stories told by children and teenagers themselves, highlighting not only their own experiences, but their venture into the dangerous disclosure/sharing arena. Their "right to be heard" is an international right:

> The right to be heard and to protection and care is declared in the UN Convention on the Rights of the Child (UNCRC). A number of articles declare children's rights, including the right to be involved in the realization of children's rights at all levels of society (United Nations). There are some studies in which COA *have* told stories about their lives. (Tinnfalt et al., 2011, p. 135) (emphasis in original)

To complicate the question of disclosure further, I again bring into the mix the Geographic Cure Child who suffers all the turmoil of being raised by an alcoholic parent, who would love and greatly benefit from involvement in a support group or one-on-one counseling time, but who *wasn't at that school* when the screenings were conducted. Or, maybe the child has self-identified, and the current school is ready to participate, but then the child promptly disappears from school because the parent has taken off again. Disclosure is difficult enough for the child who lives in one place, but there are at least possibilities for trust among the familiar adults he or she knows. Disclosure is far more difficult for the child who lives on the road with an alcoholic. There is no one to trust.

One resource for Children of Alcoholics that was not available when I was young is, of course, the Worldwide Web. There is instant community to be found on the Web: global interests to be pursued, research to be conducted, stories to be "heard," and conversations to be had, all on the Internet. Very likely, the Internet may be the single best way to provide support groups for Geographic Cure Children, because such resources transcend the physical space of the child's current school. I agree wholeheartedly with Weaver (2010) who writes, "What is lacking in curriculum conversations is technology. Without technology the 'magic of art' is nearly impossible in the posthuman condition" (p. 143). The Worldwide Web has the potential to help caring individuals reach the silent child who fears the spilling of secrets, and the Web can certainly be a place where such children can support each other. In discussing viable options for supporting Children of Alcoholics, Cuijpers (2005) in fact observed that a "relatively straightforward intervention method would be a supportive website for children of problem drinkers" (p. 473).

Fortunately, there is in fact a remarkably supportive website on the Internet now. This resource, located at shoutinginside.com, has a section titled "Whispers in the Roar" that posts stories written by teens whose parents are addicted to alcohol or drugs. Visitors to the website are told, "Check out how other people deal with a mom or dad who drinks too much or has a drug problem. You aren't alone and now you don't have to keep shouting inside" (Shouting Inside, n.d.). Designed to appeal to teenagers specifically, the blog categories under which teens can post their stories, questions, or responses include "Neglect Is My Life," "Totally Embarrassed," "Annoyed to the Highest Degree," and more. The resources linked to this website are a treasure chest full of information that caring adults *wish* they could give Children of Alcoholics. To bring awareness of Shouting Inside to teenage Children of Alcoholics is to offer a way for them to "befriend the monster" (the silent family secrets) and "let it show us its soul," as Doll (2011) puts it, rather than "push the monster farther into its saturnine depths," which is what the alcoholic parent insists upon (p. 24).

Teenagers who post their angry, hurt, scared, or tortured stories on the Shouting Inside website provide for each other a "been-there-done-that" communal spirit, as if they were all sitting in a circle, nodding, supporting each other. The stories are loaded with truth. If I were an uninformed person, I might read some of the postings and think, "Oh dear . . . this child has quite a flair for dramatics." However, I am someone who has, indeed, "been there and done that," and I can state unequivocally that these stories (and responses) reach out to others with authenticity and veracity. I did not have access to a Worldwide Web in the 1960s when the Geographic Cure had me most in its clutches, but if I had been able to "visit" such a website, I would have planted myself in the middle of it at every chance. If an educator has a desire to develop a deeper understanding of the experience of Children of Alcoholics, shoutinginside.com is an excellent place to begin. I feel that the website contributes much to an understanding of curriculum as "fermented text."

Part of my "call to action" with this book is to encourage writers of juvenile and young adult fiction to bring us more stories themed with parental alcoholism and the Geographic Cure. There should be numerous stories or memoirs published (and available as eBooks) with parental substance abuse themes that are age-appropriate for younger readers. Fiction was my lifeline, as it is for many troubled children. I could have greatly benefitted from reading stories about kids whose parents drink too much, especially if they described how those children handled their predicaments. I encourage teachers who are themselves Adult Children of Alcoholics to tell *their* tales as well, perhaps starting dialogue in unexpected places.

Even as an adult, I am always eager to read or hear about someone else's experiences of being raised in an 80-proof home. Adult Children of Alcoholics often compare "war stories" with like-minded adults. Many of those stories center around ruined family celebrations or holidays. As Hillman and Ventura (1993) observed, "You've been in therapy six years and you go back home on Thanksgiving and you open the front door and you see your family *and you are right back where you were. You feel the same as you always did!*" (p. 9) (emphasis in original). Never is this more true than in a family where alcohol prevails. There were few opportunities for me to swap stories with someone when I was young, however, which is why I suggest that we thoughtfully consider ways in which technology can help bring together this unique population of Geographic Cure Children who are living the Life Erratic, so that they can share their stories safely.

In the meantime, I encourage teachers to consider what it's like for the little Foreigner to come sheepishly into the strange country of the classroom, asking for hospitality. He/she isn't there by choice, any more than the teacher ends up with another child on the class rolls by choice. However, a perceptive, caring teacher can be the one adult with whom that child can have a significant relationship, even if he or she is not with that teacher for long. Perhaps the child will *disclose* after all.

DRIVING AWAY

An alcoholic parent's search for the Next Better Solution often results in the child being raised in a groundless manner. Dad is fired for being drunk at work, so he tells his kids that it's time to return to city life. The suburbs are abandoned for a third-floor walk-up. Dad is sure he'll do better if they can just get settled in. However, problems with neighbors (again, related to his drinking) make Dad change his tune about the city: it's dangerous and not fit for children. They move in with an uncle whose wife is *not* happy to see them. Dad is sure he'll get a handle on his drinking now, because he's with family, and the kids are safe. However, his sister-in-law drives him to drink. Dad drives his own brother away from him, and ultimately Dad moves on again, driving his kids out of the city altogether. Schools have changed for the children with each move, and now they seem to hate him as well. Everyone is being *driven away* in some form or other. Dad is perplexed and frustrated. He drinks one last round, but tomorrow, he's going to make it better. Turning over a new leaf will fix everything.

Such is the Life Erratic for Geographic Cure Children.

CHAPTER 5

"HOLD STILL"

INSET: THE LAUNDRYMAT LIZARD

As a child I was quite adept at using coin-operated washers and dryers. For years the routine was that I would hound my mother for her loose change, stockpiling dimes and quarters for the weekend wash. The various apartment complexes in which we lived in the mid-1960s sometimes had laundry facilities on site—a golden amenity. When there were no such facilities, my mother Marcia would drive us to "laundrymats" on weekends. I hated the times when we had to go by car. Marcia, who drank the "poor man's Bloody Mary" (beer and tomato juice) as soon as she got up on Saturday mornings, would put off the errand for hours. I would watch the clock. The longer the shadows grew on Saturday afternoons, the more I would be filled with dread. If we went too late in the day, my mother would be blitzed, and I was certain that I would end up disgraced at the laundrymat, then wrapped around a telephone pole on the way home.

During the nearly five years that we lived in an actual house with our step-family, there was a washer and dryer at home, which was pure luxury. We lost that perk, however, when my mother finally decided to leave the man who got violent when he drank. My mother, brother, and I were back in the world of cheap apartment complexes and laundry on the go, but with a new spin on things: I had a learner's permit, and could drive with an adult in the car. Citing the need for more driving experience, I would jump into the driver's seat for all family errands, before Marcia could get behind the wheel. In our new place, the laundry area was technically within the apartment compound, but it was quite a haul from our side of the complex, so we would load the baskets in the car and drive there. Since Marcia's drinking was at an all-time high, she soon began telling me, "Just go—" when it was time to wash clothes. This worked for me. I would grab the baskets and scram, even though I had no business driving even short distances alone.

An old, iodine-skinned woman who lived in the complex would hang out all day in the laundry area. She was the first adult I'd ever encountered who smoked more than my mother, and I quickly figured out that she also was a "drinker." The woman was well bottled every time I went in to wash clothes. I never remembered her name, but I secretly dubbed her "Liz, the Laundrymat Lizard" since, from my teenaged perspective, she seemed to be 110 years old. Liz's over-tanned skin was deeply lined and wrinkled, her voice was low and abrasive, her cough was disgusting, and she was bent over like a cane. She sat by the dryers for hours,

CHAPTER 5

reeking of booze and tobacco, staring at the old television set in the back. Liz was certainly avoiding *someone*, I thought, or else she was banished to the laundrymat *by* someone.

Other than a quick "hello," Liz and I rarely spoke. One rainy Saturday morning, however, the old woman scolded me when I came in with my baskets. She told me that when I drove up, she could see that the car's headlights were not on. She also noticed that I didn't use a turn signal when I pulled in to park. "When it's raining, you should turn on the lights," she admonished, "And use the damn blinker!" I mumbled that I'd only come from the other side of the complex, around the bend. She snapped, "Doesn't matter! Don't draw attention to yourself!" Her scolding tone startled me, and it scared me to know that she could tell I wasn't old enough to drive on my own. I nodded my head, and moved out of her way.

Liz evidently saw her admonishment as an ice-breaker, because from that point on, she talked to me nonstop. She used to show horses, and since I was horse-crazy around that time, we had something in common. However, Liz was becoming inquisitive. She started asking about my mother, triggering all of the spring-loaded barricades in my head. I was old enough be aware of social services; I did *not* want them involved with us. I was terrified of being separated from my brother. I could handle things, and Liz needed to leave us alone. My answers to Liz's questions were masterfully evasive, at first. But after a few more laundry sessions, I finally dropped my guard. No, my mother wasn't working. Yes, my dad sent child support. Yes, I was taking care of my brother. Liz never asked how much my mother drank. She already knew.

We first relocated to that apartment complex in March. Marcia's plan was that Geoff and I would finish the school year, and then we would move to Atlanta in June. In May I told Liz about the impending move. I said, "My mom wants to go to Atlanta because my uncle is there. She says we'll be near family, and then everything will be better." Liz snorted a little laugh. I was offended that she thought the plan was funny, even though I knew it was just another of Mom's Next Great Ideas. I pressed on defensively, hoping to persuade this outsider that we would be fine, hoping to convince myself that having a productive, steady, *sober* relative to rely upon would be just the ticket. "My grandmother lives in Atlanta too, so we'll get to see her a lot." Liz's snort-laugh then was more fervent. I mistook this self-recognition for scorn, so I remained huffy for a while. However, I got over it, and Liz never ratted us out to social services.

On the day Geoff and I packed up the car to leave town, I noticed Liz lurking on our side of the apartment complex, watching us. She watched us pour our mother into the passenger's side of the car of our old Falcon wagon. When I walked around to the driver's side, Liz walked over and brought her craggy, orange face close to mine. She jerked her head in my mother's direction and croaked, "Her life has gone to shit. That doesn't mean yours has to. And it doesn't mean she's a bad person." Then Liz backed away, and I missed her already. Wise Liz.

CHARLIE'S ANGEL AND MYSTICAL WHISPERS

> In telling his story truthfully, the ill person rises to the occasion.
> —Arthur Frank, *The Wounded Storyteller: Body, Illness and Ethics*

In the middle of my study of the Geographic Cure, a freight train loaded with irony thundered over me at full speed. I had just been diagnosed with anal cancer, and within days of hearing the definitive pathology results, I began investigating possibilities of going somewhere *else* for treatment. Doctors were spewing terms to me that I never imagined would take on a personal hue: "rare cancer" . . . "squamous cell carcinoma" . . . "aggressive radiation" . . . "particularly nasty chemotherapies." They lost me at "radiation." The doctors' words, glossed over with reassurances, spoke of the unfolding of treatment plans, but I heard a different voice: "Leave. Do not do this here." I am, after all, my mother's daughter. We panic, we leave. Prinze (2006) writes, "Panic is a response to an immediate physical threat. It is associated with a fight-or-flight response (fight is likely when flight is impossible). Anxiety is more anticipatory; it detects impeding danger and is associated with freezing" (p. 153). I wasn't frozen, I was packing a bag.

While several key factors contributed to my reaction to the news, one far eclipsed the others. Tumors in the anal canal wall are not routinely treated in Savannah—not by a long shot. Other cancers, yes, but *this one*—the cancer that most people had never heard of—is not the cancer we all see affecting our friends and family. Yet in what proved to be a sardonic twist, I had just witnessed a family friend's heartbreak as she had to stand by and watch anal cancer claim the life of her father. My friend and colleague Jennie, a fourth-grade teacher at my school, lost her beloved father Ken to anal cancer. Ken was treated in Savannah, his hometown for his entire life. His doctors thought they "had it," but Ken's cancer came back with a vengeance. Other organs were affected, and then it was too late. Although Jennie's parents only lived two streets away from me, I didn't really know Ken. I knew his brave wife, and I knew his lovely daughter, a phenomenal educator who tried to be strong and continue teaching even as her heart was being wrenched from her chest. When I was told soon after Ken's funeral that I had the same cancer, the chase for a cure was *on*.

Before I learned about Jennie's father, my only frame of reference regarding anal cancer was the death of an original "Charlie's Angel"—Farah Fawcett. When her death was reported in June of 2009, I was in an airport, waiting for a delayed flight. The actress's picture was on all the televisions at all of the gates: Farah, grinning that pearly white grin, confident in her fabulous tan and tank top bathing suit. The accounts of her battle made me shudder in that distant, "Oh, the poor soul" manner with which we sometimes receive news that has nothing to do with us. Newscasters explained that Farah had gone to Germany seeking alternative treatment options, and, for a short while, thought she had found her miracle cure. "She was mistaken," they announced, shaking their heads sadly. *What a loss*, I agreed, shaking my head

CHAPTER 5

just as sadly. My plane finally took off, but when I landed in my layover city, the televisions were covered with Michael Jackson's face. I learned that while I was in flight, Farah's demise had swiftly taken a back seat to Michael Jackson's death, which occurred later that day. Newscasters stopped saying the words "anal cancer" on television, and Farah's battle with such an uncommon, mysterious disease became old news.

In August of that same summer, when I returned to school, I learned that Jennie's dad Ken was being treated for *some type* of cancer. At first Jennie spoke very little about the details of her dad's cancer, but we learned that his was in the colorectal group. Most of us surmised Ken's disease to be colon cancer. Ken, who was only in his late 50s, was a husband, father, and grandfather who lived in Savannah his whole life, and whose entire family lived here as well. At the time he was fighting the disease, it never dawned on me to wonder if going somewhere else for treatment would have made a difference for Ken. I only knew that it was terribly tragic that Ken was slipping away. My heart ached watching Jennie bravely try to do her job at school while losing her father. During the winter of 2010, Ken took a serious turn for the worst. Only then did we learn that Ken was battling the same rare cancer that defeated Farah Fawcett—anal cancer. None of my co-workers, friends, or family had ever personally known or heard of anyone who had such an obscure form of cancer. Ken was buried in late March of 2010, after having lived only *one year* from the time of his diagnosis. One year! All of the staff members at my school were heartsick. "So young, so quick, so sad." "So bizarre, this rare cancer coming out of nowhere." Two months later, I was diagnosed with that same disease.

In my case, the cancer was discovered early, despite the fact that I was initially keeping quiet about my symptoms. The pain and bleeding that I had sporadically experienced that previous fall became quite consistent by January. My friend Melodie noticed that I winced when I sat down, when I was with her at a movie or in a coffee shop. She asked what was going on, and I finally stopped being dismissive and told her about the symptoms. Melodie bugged me about calling my primary physician, and I said I would. But I didn't. The symptoms were happening to me during a year when I was splitting my time between two schools. I was expected to manage the gifted programs at both an elementary school and a middle school. The work load at each was full-time, yet I was only a ".5 person" at both. I had been working very late at one school or the other, plus going in on weekends. I was more overwhelmed with work than I had been in decades. Additionally, I was mired in issues surrounding my stepmother's steep decline into Alzheimer's disease. She lived in Seattle, so I was traveling back and forth in an attempt to "handle" the situation. Adding to all that, I was trying to write this book. I was far too busy to go to a doctor.

That all changed in April, two weeks before I defended my prospectus. One day, at the elementary school where I worked, I noticed that the principal, Julie, was walking as if in pain. I asked Julie if her back hurt, and she explained quietly that she was having hemorrhoid problems. I told her that I thought the same thing was going on with me, and followed her into her office. I'd never had hemorrhoids before, and I wanted details. (Julie and I were close friends years before she became a principal; I can't imagine having such a conversation with any other "boss.") Once Julie described her "flare-ups," it seemed that I'd found a logical answer to my dilemma. When I told her what was going on with me, she agreed that our symptoms were similar. Julie began to tell me what her doctor had proposed (a surgical option) the last time she had an exam. I had to stop her. Just the word "exam" made my legs turn to Jell-O. "Oh good God," I said. "I can't have doctors examining me *there!* It would hurt! Plus, I would be *so* mortified!" What a price we put on dignity, until our lives depend upon being robbed of every shred. Cue the ominous music in the movie of my life.

Several days later I poked my head into Julie's office and asked how long "flare-ups" usually last. Julie was typing at her computer, so she answered quickly, "Oh, I'm fine now. All better." Then she stopped typing, and looked at me. Julie asked, "Are you still having problems?" When I told her that my symptoms were actually worse, not better, and that clots were involved, she went pale. "You need to go to your doctor. *Now.*" There was panic in Julie's eyes. At the time, her concern registered with me simply as empathy. *I* was thinking about the pain and mortification involved with such as appointment. *Julie* was thinking of Jennie's dad.

The next day, my longtime primary physician, internist Dr. F., insisted that I see Dr. H., a gastroenterologist, as soon as possible. She called Dr. H. herself, and asked that he see me immediately. I was an obedient patient, following through in hopes of a very simple solution—preferably in pill form, or maybe a sitz bath. At this point my symptoms had been going on nonstop for months, so upon listening to me recount my issues, Dr. H. said, "Colonoscopy. Next week." I balked. It was not yet time for a second colonoscopy. I'd had that requisite "first one" five years earlier, when I turned 50, and I wanted the full ten years, as promised, before having to go through *that* all over again. Dr. H. was adamant. "The colonoscopy will be the best way to get answers," he said. The procedure was scheduled, and papers were handed to me before I could blink.

In an uncanny twist of events, the appointment date that Dr. H.'s office assigned to me for the colonoscopy turned out to be the date that had already been scheduled for my prospectus defense. At that early point, my priorities were clear. There was no way I would ask my committee members to try to find another mutually agreeable date. Instead, I called Dr. H.'s office and made them change my appointment to the following week. I joked around with friends about the similar levels of scrutiny involved with these two examinations. Not once did I think there was any serious reason to hurry for, or worry about, the dreaded medical procedure.

My colonoscopy was on a Tuesday of the last week in April. While in the waiting room that morning, I ran into a man I knew named Eddie, the ex-husband of my treasured friend Jacquelyn, a woman who fiercely fought multiple myeloma until she died in 2003. Eddie and Jacquelyn were divorced decades before she died, but they had stayed in touch, and I'd met him a few times over the years. I had not seen Eddie since the day of Jacquelyn's funeral. Seeing him in this context—the

CHAPTER 5

gastroenterologist's office—gave me a vaguely peculiar feeling, but I attributed the weirdness to my still-acute sadness about Jacquelyn's death. Seeing Eddie naturally brought to mind my dear friend, which then prompted me to remember details of her courageous battle with cancer. Jacquelyn fought her disease kicking and screaming, never giving up for a second until death finally triumphed. I miss her every day, and seeing Eddie made me choke up a little. Looking back now at this strange encounter with my friend's ex-husband, I wonder if my resulting recollections of Jacquelyn's fierceness were a warning in some fashion. Or, more positively, a preparation. For a long time, if an image of Jacquelyn floated into my mind, it came in the form of a cancer-patient version of Rosie the Riveter: "We Can Do It!" I've never seen anyone combat illness the way Jacquelyn fought. Running into Eddie made that fond image of Jacquelyn/Rosie present herself front and center in my thoughts. Perhaps Jacquelyn herself was preparing me. I had often thought of my friend as my guardian angel, certain that she was intervening in my life on numerous occasions long before this colonoscopy.

As I was getting dressed after the procedure, I wondered if I would run into Eddie again on the way out. This thought naturally brought Jacquelyn's "Rosie" face back to my mind's eye, which is what I was seeing when the nurse came in (*We Can Do It!*) to tell me that a mass was found. The nurse gave me a sheet of color photos taken by the camera during the procedure. I couldn't make sense of the pictures, from any angle. I was groggy, so the nurse spoke primarily to my neighbor Syril, my driver for the day. She explained that although Dr. H. made several attempts to get biopsy samples from the mass during the procedure, there was too much bleeding. "He had no choice but to stop," she said. Solemnly, the nurse explained that the tissue samples that Dr. H. *did* manage to obtain from the tumor were being sent to a lab. There was a strong chance that I would be referred to Dr. X., a colorectal surgeon, she added. "Take those photos with you," she directed, as if she knew with certainty that I'd be going to the surgeon.

The term "mass" did not yet send up a flare, and frankly, the word "biopsy" rolled off my back. I've had numerous biopsies taken from various parts of my body over the years, including a couple of frightening lumps in my neck (decades ago) that doctors first assumed were symptoms of Hodgkin's Disease. In all cases, the biopsies came back negative. I stopped fretting over that word quite some time ago. This would be another one of those instances, I was certain. If the universe was trying, in some fashion, to prepare me with these Jacquelyn images, I wasn't seeing it. By that afternoon, when I had been home a while and was fully awake, I had more pressing concerns: the biopsy "attempts" left me raw and hurting. I only cared about making the pain stop.

Dr. H. called me the next morning and carefully explained the situation. He said that the mass *might* just be a thrombosed hemorrhoid, containing a blood clot on the inside. He warned me, however, that they would not trust a negative lab report from his biopsy attempts. "If it's negative, we will send you to Dr. X. so that he can perform an excisional biopsy at the hospital, while you're under anesthesia."

Dr. H. said that if the tissue samples that he had previously managed to take came back positive for cancer, those results *would* count. "That will at least save you the pain of that excisional biopsy. You would just move ahead with next steps." *Terrific*, I remember thinking, in my cluelessness. *With my luck, the results will come back negative, and they'll make me go through this surgical thing, only to prove that the mass is nothing serious.* The reference to "next steps" went right past me. I wasn't worried about the "mass" or any next steps. I was worried about being inflicted with more reasons to hurt. And I was aggravated that the situation was dragging out.

My husband Andreas and I both felt that this would be another false alarm—just one more thing biopsied, to be on the safe side. I always thought that if I ever had cancer, I would *know*. I'd sense it, maybe even before doctors performed tests. Instead, there was no such internal foreshadowing. Rather, I searched the Internet for information about thrombosed hemorrhoids, wanting to become an informed patient, certain that this mass would turn out to be something akin to *those things*—benign, albeit weird. I couldn't have cancer, surely, because I didn't *feel* as though I had cancer. I couldn't have been running errands, working insane hours, laughing, doing laundry, finishing a doctoral program, moving through time, without knowing something was wrong. Most assuredly I would have known it, would have felt in my soul somewhere that cancer had invaded my body. Therefore, this thing, whatever it was, would prove to be just a fluke. Joan Didion (2005) describes how the "unthinkable" comes without warning:

> It was in fact the ordinary nature of everything preceding the event that prevented me from truly believing it had happened, absorbing it, incorporating it, getting past it. I recognize now that there was nothing unusual in this: confronted with sudden disaster we all focus on how unremarkable the circumstances were in which the unthinkable occurred, the clear blue sky from which the plane fell, the routine errand that ended on the shoulder with the car in flames, the swings where the children were playing as usual when the rattlesnake struck from the ivy. (pp. 3–4)

I tried to go back to work while waiting for the pathology report on the tissue samples that Dr. H. managed to obtain. All the schools in our system were in the middle of the asinine (in my opinion) state-mandated criterion-referenced test; it was a terrible time for any staff member to be out. All hands on deck, so to speak. The principal of the middle school, where I was supposed to be for half of each week, gave me permission to remain at the elementary school (near my house) each day during the "testing window." This kept me from having to drive to the other side of town while in pain. Julie was just as understanding, taking my name off of all test administrator and proctor lists. I tried to help instead with checking tests out to teachers, getting the next day's tests in order, etc.

Two days after the colonoscopy, Dr. H. tracked me down by phone with news: The biopsy attempts that he took came back negative. My first reaction was wild relief. Since the state tests were being administered up and down the hallway,

CHAPTER 5

I couldn't whoop and holler, but I was delighted. *"Woo-Hoo! I knew it!!"* He then added, "Remember, this doesn't mean we have a true negative. It may mean that my samples weren't conclusive enough. Remember I had to stop before I could get what we needed. You'll need to go see Dr. X. on Friday and set up an excisional biopsy." *Okay sure. Whatever. One more hoop to jump through.*

Fortified with optimism, I anticipated that the appointment with the colorectal surgeon would be perfunctory. It would go something like this: Dr. X. would explain what the biopsy would entail. I would stress how poorly I've always handled anesthesia after surgeries in my past (becoming violently ill upon waking). Dr. X. would reassure me that newest anti-nausea medications would make all the difference. He would tell me about follow-up care and would approve of the special cushion I'd already bought. I would have my calendar with me, and we'd set up the date and time for the outpatient surgical procedure. We would shake hands. *Piece of cake visit.* That's how I this appointment would play out, I was certain. To me, the phrase "set up the biopsy" implied that I would sit through an informational session, and then lock in a date.

Andreas was teaching Advanced Placement Physics, and because it was close to the time for the A.P. exams, I discouraged him from planning to go to this visit with me. Certainly, he didn't need to take time off just to go with me to a mundane set-up-the-biopsy appointment. And there was no need for any friend to go along with me to the appointment, either. I could drive, even though it was quite uncomfortable to do so. The appointment was simply an information-gathering and biopsy-scheduling session, I assumed. *What else could it be?* This line of reasoning is why I went to meet Dr. X. alone that Friday. And this is when fate finally pierced my self-protective bubble and *the unthinkable* slashed through my heart.

THE KEN FACTOR

Before going to Dr. X.'s office, I stopped by my school to take care of a few pressing matters. Jennie was in the office, so I told her that I was being sent to Dr. X., wondering if she knew anything about him. She said, "He was my dad's surgeon! Dr. X. is the best." I felt badly about prompting Jennie to think about her dad, and hoped I hadn't caused the rest of her day to be difficult. However, I was happy to hear that she liked this doctor. I felt no unease about my upcoming session with Ken's surgeon. Denial provides an impenetrable force field against clarity. Rather than feeling any glint of fear, I felt only sadness for Jennie.

Upon meeting Dr. X. later that day, I mentioned that I knew he had been one of Ken's doctors. I said, "I'm a friend of Jennie's. We teach at the same school." Dr. X. smiled at the mention of Jennie, but then shook his head sadly and said, "Yeah, tough case. Ken was such a great guy. We all loved him." Dr. X. then asked me about my symptoms. Within minutes, he stood up to leave the room, telling me first to pull down my pants and lie sideways on the table, so that he could perform an exam. He would return in a minute. I was *stunned* but had no time to react. Dr. X.'s nurse helped me up on the table and onto my side. Then she came around to the side I was facing to grab my hand. She said she was sorry that I had no warning about being examined, but the doctor needed to inspect the tumor before planning the surgery. *Wait! I have pictures from the colonoscopy!* That unexpected exam became the first of countless, beyond-humiliating, painful probings that became (and still are, even at this writing) par for the course.

Pain and humiliation are sinister bedfellows. I sputtered out heavy profanity and blubbered like a two-year-old. I was still raw from the colonoscopy biopsy attempts and did not expect any other disturbances in that general area before the day of the surgical biopsies. When the exam was finally over, Dr. X. left the room so that I could get dressed and pull myself together. What an appropriate image: "pull yourself together." Difficult, when one is completely coming unglued. Mensch (2005) writes:

> The notion of self-control implies a division in our selfhood between the components that control and those that are controlled. . . . Each component seems to have its own claims to rule. This, at least, is the conclusion that can be drawn from Freud's final account of the id, the superego, and the ego. (p. 121)

The nurse, who had been handing me tissues, finally just gave me the box. I believe, now, that the crying came from a deeper place of knowing. However, I finally managed to shove that *knowing* back into its dark corner for a tiny bit longer. I composed myself. Ready to be given the particulars about the excisional biopsies, I pulled my calendar and pen out of my purse, and waited. Surely the worst was over.

When Dr. X. returned, his facial expression projected incredulity. He shook his head slowly in amazement and said quietly, "It's wild that you mentioned Ken, because I think you have the exact same thing. This is uncanny, because anal cancer is rare . . ." Dr. X. was so blown away by his discovery of such an improbable coincidence that he didn't seem to realize that *he was telling me I had cancer.* I was expecting no such news at this appointment. He talked about how much of the mass he would try to take out the following Monday (as much as possible without going too far into the wall), and how quickly he thought he could get lab results back (Wednesday). He steamrolled right on over the devastating implications. Since I was pretty much "cried out" at that point, I actually stayed calm. I asked Dr. X. if it were possible that the mass could be a thrombosed hemorrhoid instead of a tumor. He replied, "Sure, it's possible . . ." But the aura surrounding him maintained, "*Not on your life.*"

I propelled myself out of that room and up to the receptionist out front, paid my bill, and shuffled out. I walked to my car without crumbling into a heap on the asphalt. I did not call my husband, or drive to his school, even though the doctor's office was very nearby. In part, I didn't try to reach him because he was still teaching. However, the larger reason was that Andreas lost both his mother and his sister to cancer; it seemed better not to tell him about Dr. X.'s off-hand remark. Anger overcame shock by the time I reached my car. I was furious that Dr. X. would be so callous. He was

CHAPTER 5

rude to think out loud like that, about this *alleged* coincidence. I decided that visions of medical journal publication must have danced in his head, and then I became even angrier. Dr. X. had no proof. He should have kept his unsolicited pre-pathology opinion to himself. I was overwhelmed by emotion, but at that point the emotion surfacing was only anger. I wasn't afraid, *yet*. There was no urge to flee, *yet*. Instead, I found myself lit up by the hot, red glow of fury. I wanted more than just to prove to Dr. X. how very wrong he was. Prinze (2006) explains that "emotions are not really output states. They are not action commands. They are, however, perceptions of the body's preparation for action" (p. 228). The action I was preparing for was war. I wanted Dr. X.'s head on a platter.

As I started the car, my cell phone rang. The caller was my pal Julie D., a woman whose friendship I value greatly, even though clashing schedules of late had kept us from getting together very often. I was astonished that Julie D. called at the very moment that I was ingesting Dr. X.'s pronouncement. We had not spoken on the phone for months. There were only two local friends of mine who weren't working full time anymore, and Julie D. was one of them. She didn't expect me to answer—she thought I'd be working, and planned to leave a message of encouragement. She had learned from a mutual friend that I was supposed to see the surgeon, but had no idea that I'd just completed that visit. I was immensely grateful to hear her voice. While attempting to tell my friend what Dr. X. said, I became too upset. Since I was already in my car, my friend asked if I could calm down enough to drive, and meet her somewhere. She was running errands, so we agreed to meet in one of the sitting areas inside the mall. I have no memory of driving there, but I arrived safely. I found Julie D. at the designated spot and began again to tell her the story.

As I sobbed my way through the unexpected-exam part of the story, I was astonished to see Katherine, my *one other friend who wasn't working that day*. Katherine spotted me, and walked toward us, intending to just say a quick hello. She and Julie D. did not know each other, and Katherine didn't want to intrude. However, once Katherine realized that I was upset, she sat down on the other side of me and grabbed my other hand. My bookend friends kept me from falling to pieces as I launched into the full account of Dr. X.'s exams and startling comments. They were as furious as I was, and I felt better, safer, upon hearing them agree with me. "He really is nuts," we all agreed. "We will all unload on him with both barrels regarding his atrocious bedside manner, when this is over." Any plans that these two women had that afternoon fell by the wayside. My pals stayed right beside me, as if neither one had any other place to be. It amazes me that both buddies of mine were instantly placed in my path when I left Dr. X. in tears. I wonder if Jacquelyn, in her guardian angel role, steered them both in my direction. Perhaps it was just a coincidence. I have mixed feelings about coincidences, but I certainly had no intention of becoming one for Dr. X. to talk about on the golf course. Ken died one year after his first visit with Dr. X. I could not imagine doing the same. As Mensch (2005) said, "Death is, by definition, on the other side of everything I can think and know" (p. 168). I resented being grouped, by Dr. X., with Ken-who-died.

My two friends sat with me in that spot for almost two hours. They let me sob, they let me seethe with anger, and when they were sure I was not shaking anymore, they let me drive home.

I did not tell my husband the whole story that day. I told him about the surprise exam, and about the expectations for the Monday biopsy. I was resolved to keep quiet about Dr. X.'s cryptic comments. There was no sense in needlessly alarming anyone in my family. I would tell them all later, when it would become The Big Scare Over Nothing story. They would join Katherine and Julie D. in being equally enraged on my behalf that this doctor would make such a groundless comment to my face. Over that weekend I again searched the Internet, clinging to any information that explained what else a "mass" in the anal canal wall could be, besides cancer. I couldn't wait for Dr. X. to be proven wrong.

During the excisional biopsy the following Monday morning, Dr. X. took out a significant chunk of the tumor while I was out cold with anesthesia. As soon as I woke up, the pain nearly put me back out. Pain is such a *mighty* distractor; there was little room for fear. For the next few days I would list to one side in my recliner like an old frigate, or just lay on my side in the bed, trying to keep weight off my backside. I felt as though I kept sitting on one of those spikey balls from a sweet gum tree. I was distressed to learn, by trial and error, that I could not tolerate any of the pain medicines prescribed—I had horrendous reactions to them all. My body appeared to reject everything that was intended to help. Narcotic pain meds made me severely nauseated, dizzy, hot, and agitated. They also made me feel like a ninja was karate-chopping my throat. I spent much time on the phone with the doctors and my local pharmacist, as we tried various combinations of anti-nausea and pain drugs. There was no time to focus on the larger implications of what that "mass" might be. I just wanted to stop being seasick and put an end to "the tight throat thing." I finally stopped taking any pain medications and stuck to Tylenol.

On Wednesday I stared at the phone, wondering how the results would come to me. Will I have to go back Dr. X.'s office? Will they tell me, "Please come back to discuss the pathology report . . ."? If they do that, they might as well just say it.

Late that afternoon, a subdued Dr. X. called. "Ms. Nissen, it *is* cancer." *Bastard.* A black hole sucked all of the air out of the room, making sure it went nowhere near my lungs. I could feel myself sucking in myriad short breaths, but couldn't actually get any air. Oddly, I didn't cry. I asked one question: "What do I do now?" Dr. X. told me that I'd have to go the next morning to have PET and CAT scans done. I was also scheduled for separate appointments with Dr. Y., an oncologist, and Dr. Z., a radiologist. My treatment would involve aggressive chemotherapy and radiation, he explained, but no surgery. That was supposed to make me feel better. "These doctors are very good—they were Ken's doctors." *Ken's doctors.* The words hissed around the edges of the black hole. *I don't want to see Ken's doctors. I don't want to be dead in a year.* I felt weak and defenseless. There was no ability to stick up for myself. *No. Send me somewhere else.* I couldn't make myself say it. Inexplicably, I instead tried switching to convince-myself mode. *Theses doubts are unreasonable. Ken's cancer*

CHAPTER 5

wasn't caught as early as mine. Every case is different. Logic didn't do a thing for me, however. I didn't want Ken's doctors, period. Anal cancer is rare. Doctors in this town had barely treated anyone for my cancer.

My cancer. The term no one wants to own. No, no, no, this was all wrong. I'm the one who stands *next* to the cancer patient while she signs in at the appointment desk. That's my role: helper bee. *My mother. My sister-in-law.* I'm the caregiver. They sign in. I hold the purse. *Jacquelyn.* I'm the diversion, the amusement, the person who lets the cancer patient be herself. No false fronts. Lay it on me, baby. I'm the support network. *Other friends, and other friends' husbands and mothers and fathers.* What can I do to help? Other people. Their cancer. Not mine. *But it's mine now.*

This time I did call my husband at school. *Come home now.* With one short sentence, I told him everything, just as, with one phone call from Dr. X., the "area" of multiple excisional biopsies became a malignant, malicious tumor. There was still outrageous pain, so I was still on my side as much as possible. When Andreas arrived, he stretched out on the bed beside me and we talked for a while. My fear of treatments came in a rush. The realization of what a supreme chicken I was did not fare well with me, but there it was. Rosie the Riveter had skipped town. I told Andreas, "I'm not as afraid of dying as I am of hurting."

As my husband and I talked, I became engulfed in the need to leave the house. Cancer was seeping into my home, and I wasn't prepared to handle it. I couldn't face calling family or friends. I couldn't even face my own four walls. I was standing face-to-face with the same classic Geographic Cure mode that dominated my life for so long: When the going gets tough, run away! Driving away from the house, we saw Debbie, my good friend and doctoral program buddy, heading toward us. I had not called Debbie, but she was aware that I would probably hear from the surgeon that day. Andreas and I had just made a pact that for one night, we would avoid *the telling.* Therefore, we stopped the car, but all I said to Debbie was that we were headed to Barnes & Noble. She saw the rest of the story with one look at my face. Debbie *knew.* We drove on to the bookstore, where I sat leaning to one side, flipping through *The New Yorker* to look at cartoons. Two weeks prior to that night, I was typing up the notes I'd written during my prospectus defense. I was making a plan for summer: finish. But on this night, I was sitting on a pillow in Barnes & Noble, trying to digest my new summer plan: "aggressive" chemotherapy and the daily charbroiling of my behind. I called Debbie the next morning to say, "Yep, it's bad."

In addition to calling my family and closest friends that next day, I called Jennie, Ken's daughter. "Tell me everything." Jennie told me that the two chemos that work best against anal cancer are 5FU (Fluorouracil) and Mitomycin. However, her father didn't get those chemos at first, because there was a national shortage. *See? Every case is different. That was then, this is now.* Jennie's mother, who was nearby, heard her daughter answering my questions. "Tell Leslie there still is a shortage." *Holy crap.*

For the rest of that week, I was in and out of waiting rooms, exam rooms, and labs. I cried a lot at these appointments. The physical, surreal act of signing in at each reception desk was a uniquely crushing aspect of being a newly diagnosed patient. Signing in was too concrete to bear. Each time I wrote my name, reality glared back at me in black and white. It was as if I were spelling out L-e-s-l-i-e N-i-s-s-e-n h-a-s c-a-n-c-e-r, every time. I also cried because I was physically hurting. Getting into and out of a car was torture, because it killed me to sit or twist toward another direction. What enabled me to push myself through those appointments was my desperate need for information. And there certainly were floods of information. During these early visits I learned that anal cancer is *quite* different from the much more common colorectal cancer. The "mass" they found—the malignant tumor in the anal canal wall—was created by the abnormal and uncontrolled growth of cancer cells. Many cancers are fought with a two-pronged attack out of three choices: surgery, chemotherapy, and radiation. In my case, there would be no further surgery after the hacking away at the tumor that had already occurred during the excisional biopsies. My weapons would be chemotherapy and radiation. As I was carried along by the current of information, doctor appointments, orientations, and lab visits, the experience felt like the early days following a death in the family: There is so much to do that you can't spend time thinking about that thing that you don't want to think about.

There was "much to do" at home as well. When I wasn't trying to sleep, I was on my little glass porch, hanging over the side of my recliner, watching neighbors and birds while I talked on the phone to loved ones who were spread out across the country. I emailed more friends and family, and talked with people who stopped by. Andreas left the kitchen door unlocked and put up a note: "Come on in. Leslie's on the porch." A few friends who came over made me laugh, which was a marvel. A few others couldn't help crying. Friends from work were especially frightened, because The Ken Factor loomed over us all. *Dead in a year.*

While waiting to hear the results of those scans, I sporadically made mental lists: Child-Raising Tips for Sam and His (Future) Wife / Family Stories to Preserve. There were countless "To-Do" lists in my head: Clean Out Closets / Decide How Jewelry Will be Distributed Among Relatives and Friends / Ask Georgia Southern if Honorary Degrees Can be Awarded Posthumously. The moments when I could not imagine a future for myself were quiet and cold. Grudin (1982) writes, "Calm people swim freely into the future and speak of it as if it were part of them. But those who are hopeless for reasons of age or grief or illness barely use the future tense at all; and for frightened people the future can shrink to almost nothing" (p. 98). It's difficult to keep hopelessness at bay when cancer slithers in. Jennie's dad—dead in a year.

Once the PET and CAT scan results were in, the future peeked up over the wall. The cancer was confined to the tumor—it had not spread. A deluge of relief washed over me. As soon as those results were in, it was time to face the official treatment orientation appointments with the oncologist and radiologist recommended by Dr. X. My primary physician, Dr. F., deferred to the surgeon's selection of those particular doctors because they did, at least, have *some* kind of experience with anal cancer.

CHAPTER 5

Dr. F. was completely honest with me: I was the first and (as of this writing) *only* patient of hers to be diagnosed with anal cancer. She had no local frame of reference to go by in terms of treatment recommendations.

At that point Dr. F. and I did not discuss the possibility of my going elsewhere. We were wrapped up in trying to find a combination of pain medicine and anti-nausea medicine that would not cause an allergic reaction. Therefore, Andreas and I did indeed end up in the offices of Ken's doctors, these "physicians of coincidence," because no other option was offered. The orientation and new-patient visits were conducted separately. We did not get to see the oncologist and radiologist together, in the same room at the same time, yet I was expected to consider them my *team*. Dr. Y. had both my PET and CAT scan reports, but Dr. Z. had only one. Dr. Z. remembered my medicine allergies, Dr. Y. did not. Dr. Z. warned me, "You'll have a bitch of a summer," then had me return for a separate orientation to the radiation area itself. His technicians made me lie on my back so that they could make a fiberglass mold of my backside, which would be used to keep me in a quite unnatural position during radiation: frog-legged, feet touching but knees far apart, heels way up close to my crotch. This position killed my hip bones as well as my behind. To lie that way under any circumstances would be uncomfortable, but to be in that position after having the biopsies was excruciating: the position forced me to put pressure on the excisional site. "Every time you come in, you'll get back into this position with the mold," a technician explained cheerfully. I dreamed, later, of sledgehammers and fiberglass splinters.

There was so much pain that I could not fathom the thought of letting them begin radiation. Neither doctor inspired me to channel Jacquelyn or Rosie the Riveter. There was no *I Can Do It!* feeling. The two doctors instilled only fear and dread, which germinated finally into: *What do* they *know?* Not only did I want a second opinion, but I wanted it to come from a major cancer center, rather than from another physician in Savannah. In fact, the only ironclad feeling of strength that I could muster at that point was that determination to *go elsewhere* before talking to any other doctors about treatment options. As Audre Lorde (1997) describes:

> I needed to rally my energies in such a way as to image myself as a fighter resisting rather than as a passive victim suffering. At all times, it felt crucial to me that I make a conscious commitment to survival. (p. 75)

Certainly, I wanted to make that commitment, but I couldn't. *Not there.* I just wasn't sure that inexperienced physicians were in the best position to help me. I was mired in helpless victim muck. I felt defeated upon learning that Dr. X. had been right all along.

My second-opinion quest was not about confirming the presence of cancer. The pathology report and PET and CAT scans were certainly proof enough. The original mission was to find out if specialists with vast experience in *my cancer* would endorse the treatment plan outlined for me by the local doctors. The cancer facilities I'd heard of in the past were at Duke University in North Carolina, Sloan-Kettering in New York City, MD Anderson in Houston, and the Mayo Clinics in Minnesota and Florida. Serendipity, however, created an offer that I couldn't refuse.

THE GOLDEN OPTION

The several-day time span of scans, treatment orientations, and butt-mold fittings coincided with my son Sam's last few days of law school in Cambridge, Massachusetts. Plans had only just recently been put into place for us to attend Sam's graduation. Airline tickets had been purchased, and the hotel room was booked. I find it rather remarkable that these plans were set at the last minute, just barely before I was diagnosed. Originally, Sam was determined to skip the graduation ceremonies altogether. He was not interested in the traditional pomp and circumstance surrounding the event, nor in the expense required for his family to attend. I respected Sam's wishes and appreciated his concerns about the cost, even though I was disappointed. However, a few weeks before commencement and *just* before my need for a colonoscopy surfaced, Sam asked if I truly had been wishing he would jump through those ceremonial hoops. I answered honestly: "Yes, I would, in fact, love to see my son graduate from Harvard Law School." Sam signed up for graduation at the last possible second. I joyfully bought our airline tickets. My husband's trip would put him in Boston just in time for the graduation ceremony itself. But my itinerary began on the Monday of graduation week, so that I could attend any university or friend activities in which Sam was willing to participate.

Once the colonoscopy took place, of course, everything went to hell. Before I knew it, I was telling my son over the phone that I had cancer. I didn't want to inform him in that manner, but there was little choice. There were still a couple of weeks in between the diagnosis and graduation, and I was afraid he would hear my news from one of his Savannah contacts. (Word was spreading quickly, due to the novelty of the cancer.) How disheartening, to have to call my son while he's writing his very last law school papers and studying for finals, to tell him such news. After a couple of stunned conversations, Sam and I tried to focus subsequent phone calls on the happy occasion of his graduation. I was thrilled that Sam made that last-minute decision to "walk." I wonder, now, if Jacquelyn had been whispering in his ear.

Meanwhile, during the grueling appointments with the Savannah doctors, I made it clear that I did not want to start treatment until after that trip to Boston. There was no way I would cancel plans to see Sam graduate. *Especially now.* Even if it would kill me to sit on the plane, I wanted desperately to be there. They acquiesced, but made it clear that I had to start my treatments the very next week. While I was moving, dazed, through that revolving door of medical visits and detail-gathering, my son spent his last few days doing not only his own work, but research of another kind. Sam knew I wanted to go elsewhere for a second opinion, so he began an exhaustive cancer treatment inquiry. He called all the major cancer centers in the U.S. with a number of very specific questions, which he asked of every facility. The two questions that counted the most were, "How many anal cancer patients have you treated with radiation?" and, "What is your long-term success rate?" Sam created a spreadsheet so that the answers could be compared, side by side. A few facilities emerged as top referral hospitals for anal cancer. The positive responses and impressive success rate data from Massachusetts General Hospital (MGH) in Boston put that facility on the short list of the top three treatment centers. And I already had an airline ticket to be in Boston in a few days. *Could this work?* The trip might result in my finding an excellent second-opinion option, *if* I could get in to see a doctor with less than a week's notice.

When I called Massachusetts General Hospital, everyone with whom I spoke jumped to attention, making it their own priority to make the appointment happen. Could I fax records immediately? Yes. Could I obtain the actual pathology slides taken from the tumor, and "overnight" them to Boston? Absolutely (even if I have to break in to a lab to get them). Could I get to MGH by Tuesday morning? Without a doubt. I was captivated by the fact that my arrival in Boston was already scheduled for Monday night. This time around, I loved coincidences. Then, by what seemed to me to be an outright miracle, I was given an appointment to see Dr. Hong, the director of radiation oncology for gastrointestinal cancers, *and* Dr. Kwak (rhymes with "rock"), the gastrointestinal oncologist, together. Both doctors in the same room at the same time—something I couldn't make happen in Savannah. I already liked Massachusetts General and I hadn't even left home yet.

And I was, undeniably, experiencing the strongest of urges to leave home. *Home* means something totally different to me now, in my 50s, than it did when I was growing up, or even in my younger adult life. After living in so many different cities and states for the first 27 years of my life, I have remained in Savannah for the last 31 years. More remarkably—considering all the moves I made with my mother within the same part of town, and even the moves I made as an adult within Savannah when I first lived here—I now can say that I have lived in the very same house for the last 22 years. My house is *home*, and from the core of my being, I did not want cancer invading my home. *Home* is family, friends, warmth, laughter. *Cancer* is the unwelcome trespasser who should not be allowed to cross my threshold. Arthur Kleinman (1998) describes cancer "an unsettling reminder of the obdurate grain of unpredictability and uncertainty and injustice—value questions, all—in the human condition" (p. 20). Yes, pig-headed unpredictability, my old nemesis. I begged to differ. I also could not tolerate the idea of lying in a sickbed, having friends and coworkers visit to pat me on the hand. *Who needs to see what I am likely to become during treatment?* The two prongs of attack were not only going to be aggressive and brutal individually, but would collide with each other as well. The chemotherapy drugs involved would wreak havoc on my GI tract, which, at the same time, was going to be fried. I was not sure I could do it at all, and most assuredly could not picture myself going home to my much-loved porch after every treatment.

Some people feel strongly about preferring to die at home. Not me. I want to wander away from the pack and leave my home untouched. The physical space I called "home" changed so often in my life that I am quite territorial about where I live now.

The Spanish language has a lovely word for a favorite, safe place: *"querencia."* Our little glass porch is my favorite room in the house, and it was *not* going to become a sick room. Cancer would *not* be allowed to change the dynamics of my *querencia*.

Such thoughts began to gel into a plan, as the importance of a second-opinion "visit" began to morph into something more critical. I finally could name what I wanted: a second-option-for-*treatment*, period, away from home. Just the knowledge that I would be talking to doctors in Boston gave me strength. I spent a little time at school, with my selfless neighbor acting as my chauffeur, to wrap up some things before leaving that Monday. I had a feeling, or more accurately, a hope, that I might not be back for a long while. While at school, I found my friend Jennie and asked if her dad had considered going somewhere else for a second opinion. She told me that he did not. Ken wanted to stay in Savannah for treatment and be near his wife, children, and grandchildren. He was not at all interested in going away from home for treatment. "We all wish Dad had gone to Emory in Atlanta, or down to the Mayo Clinic in Jacksonville, or *somewhere*," Jennie said. "But he wouldn't budge. Maybe you're supposed to learn from that."

NAMING IT, CLAIMING IT

Jennie and I had more than second opinions to talk about, however. As the updates about *my cancer* spread, so did the ridiculous and futile conjectures about how I ended up with the disease. Although my good friends never wasted time with such ponderings, there were others who harbored ill-conceived notions about how one "gets" anal cancer. Jennie told me that this happened with her dad, as well, which is one reason why, at work, we were not initially told which type of cancer Ken had. Cursory Google searches were turning up "profiles" about anal cancer patients' lifestyles: *Anal sex. Multiple sex partners at a young age.* Those were not my histories, nor were they Ken's. But who looks past the first few Google results that pop up? One non-friend's web search displayed information linking some anal cancer tumors to melanoma. She asked me if I sunbathed in the nude. *Oh yeah, right. I lie on my stomach at the beach, and aim my bare behind way up toward the sun. I like a* complete *tan.*

These presumptions about hypothetical "causes" of my cancer infiltrated only a small number of conversations with people, but those instances nevertheless left a lasting scar. While offering flimsy words of encouragement, their unasked questions hovered about like gnats. Fortunately, 98% of the colleagues, neighbors, and acquaintances who offered support and prayers to me were sincere. I decided quickly that the other two percent, cloaked in the ignorance of superficial Internet searches and whispers, could kiss the very same cancer-invaded ass that they were wondering about. I did not *deserve* this cancer. No one *deserves* to become ill. Cancer victim Audre Lorde (1997) wrote in her journal:

> The idea that the cancer patient should be made to feel guilty about having had cancer, as if in some way it were all her fault for not having been in the right

CHAPTER 5

> psychological frame of mind at all times to prevent cancer, is a monstrous distortion of the idea that we can use our psychic strengths to help heal ourselves. This guilt trip which many cancer patients have been led into (you see, it is a shameful thing because you could have prevented it if only you had been more . . .) is an extension of the blame-the-victim syndrome. (p. 76)

Who knows why cancer becomes the Foreigner, invading the body at will? I became a Foreigner to myself as the "sick me" encroached upon the home country of the "formerly well me." The sick me was *not* offered hospitality in the manner Derrida (2000) describes. Yet, I will never know why the unwelcome guest tried to take up residence in my body. Certainly, I had thoughts about blame, but the arrows were targeted outward. Did working at two schools make me sick? Did Diet Coke make me sick? Did my autobiographical, psychoanalytic examination of fermented parenting and Geographic Cure Children make me sick? How freakishly Freudian to "grow" a pain in the ass while writing about being raised by one. If there were any link at all between my cancer and my various childhood or teenaged traumas (which is doubtful) the connection would not be related to writing about them, but to living for years with an internalized parent carrying on her toxic work within me, as Alice Miller (2005) describes. If that is the case, how fortunate for me that I've learned from Marla Morris how to examine my life through a psychoanalytic lens. And I've learned that, as Miller (2005) explains, "we must listen seriously to what our bodies are telling us" (p. 132). I broke the taboo. I talked about it. The poison is gone now.

Although anal cancer is often linked to HPV (the human papilloma virus), I will never know conclusively how I ended up with the disease. I decided early on that trying to pinpoint the cause of my cancer was a waste of energy that could be spent on healing. My loved ones felt the same way. Friends and colleagues who were not second-guessing the *why* of my cancer still had a hard time saying the name of my disease out loud. I empathize now with what it must have been like for breast cancer patients years ago, when no one would say *that* term out loud. When my diagnosis first slapped me in the face, my initial instinct had been to keep very quiet about the disease. Keeping secrets is second nature to Children of Alcoholics; we are quite accustomed to keeping our turmoil to ourselves, away from meddling eyes and ears. However, I chose instead to step out of the silence. Like Lorde (1997), I did not want "my anger and pain and fear about cancer to fossilize into yet another silence, nor to rob me of whatever strength can lie at the core of this experience, openly acknowledged and examined" (p. 7). This was not always easy. Even amongst my closest friends and loved ones, there were some who could not bring themselves to say the words "anal cancer." They would call it colorectal cancer, or say "the tumor is in her behind . . ." Remarkably, reticence on their part contributed to a corresponding increased determination on my part to name it, and talk about it. There were some awkward moments with a handful of coworkers and parents of students, whose prickly countenance made me feel defensive. Discussing "the shame of being ill," Morris (2008) writes, "In American culture, illness is not something to be talked about. Illness is shunned.... The teacher is supposed to embody health and knowledge. Knowledge is supposed to come from a healthy body, not from a sick one" (p. 69). I felt as though that small number of people were as glad to see me leave town as I was. Fortunately, a much larger number of friends, co-workers, neighbors and, of course, family members, made me feel tremendously loved, not shamed.

I certainly did leave town, though, within two weeks of the conclusive diagnosis. Before I could even heal from the excisional biopsies, I was already on a plane, traveling far up the Atlantic Coast, hoping to find The Great and Powerful Something Better. This was when that freight train full of irony flattened me, thundering right over my cancer-invaded body. I realized that once again, I was the subject of a live portrait—a living, breathing, and this time *literal* depiction of the search for a Geographic Cure. Only this time, *I* was the one slumped against a window, and an airline pilot was doing the "driving." I was traveling a thousand miles away because out *there*, away from *here*, was the fix. It seems that the Geographic Cure was embedded in my DNA.

THE DOCTOR, THE CAPE, AND THE RED LETTER "S"

During the second-opinion visit at Massachusetts General Hospital, light came streaming back into my heart. In the examination room, I experienced the single most significant event in this cancer saga: I channeled my own Rosie the Riveter. After spending a mere 30 minutes with Dr. Hong and Dr. Kwak, a river of courage rushed through my veins. *I* Can *Do It!* There was something reassuring about those two doctors' confidence (not cockiness), which stemmed from their having decades of experience with *my cancer.* My son was with me, and he felt encouraged as well. I asked how often MGH patients stay in remission. Dr. Hong said, "Over 95% never have a recurrence. You won't be in remission. You'll be cured." I then asked about the shortage of the two chemotherapy drugs used for anal cancer. Both doctors blinked at me. "We never have a shortage here," Dr. Kwak said. "We're a referral hospital for anal cancer. People from all over the world come here. Our pharmacy keeps the two drugs in stock." *Oh, Ken, I'm so sorry.* Relief and survivor guilt—a bewildering combination.

At various points in our talk, Dr. Hong would begin a sentence with "If you were my patient . . ." These were not offhand remarks. He was being very specific about how he would be doing things differently for me. With my medical records in his hands, he thumbed through pages and said, "I don't see the results from a pelvic MRI. Have you had one?" When I said I had not, I saw a glance shoot between Dr. Hong and Dr. Kwak: fleeting, but palpable. He continued, "If you were my patient, I would send you for the pelvic MRI right away." In five more instances, Dr. Hong or Dr. Kwak noted differences in how decisions would be made about my treatment. They were surprised to hear that in the days since the excisional biopsies, the Savannah radiologist had not performed an exam to feel the tumor. I told them

CHAPTER 5

that Dr. Z. started to do an exam (I thought he was just trying to look, not *feel*) but he stopped, because I was so torn up from the biopsies, and in so much pain. Dr. Hong said that he would have stopped too . . . *however*, he would have explained to me that he needed to feel the tumor as soon as I could stand it. Dr. Z. simply proceeded to create my radiation plan. Dr. Hong said that such an exam is as critical as the pelvic MRI results. Both are needed for the radiologist to get a clear picture of the exact size of the tumor. At Massachusetts General, the radiation oncologist would never make a radiation plan for a patient until those two criteria were met. "If you were my patient, there would be no radiation plan for you at this time," Dr. Hong said. Dr. Kwak nodded her head in agreement. For me, it was as if his white coat opened up to reveal a big, red letter "S" on his chest, while a red cape flowed behind him. I looked at my son, pointed to Dr. Hong, and said, "I want *him*. I'm staying here."

With that pronouncement, I became an MGH patient on the spot. I had not even talked to my husband, but I knew he would want whatever made me feel most confident. Dr. Hong sent Sam out of the room and felt the tumor for himself. The exam almost killed me, but I wanted Dr. Hong to get his "clear picture." He asked the scheduling clerk to set up the pelvic MRI for the end of the week, asking her to steer clear of graduation, which was Thursday. The clerk processed all of my information, and obtained approval from my insurance company, before we left the office that day. I would come back that Friday for the MRI and another discussion with Dr. Hong; he would then discuss with me his assessment of the tumor size.

That Thursday, standing on a curb, watching the Harvard Law School Class of 2010 proceed on their "walk" through the campus, I realized how erratic my life still was, even this late in my life. One minute I'm shoving books off the dining room table to make a space for dinner. The next minute a doctor is crawling up inside of me to ascertain the exact size of a malignant tumor. In one more minute I'm as happy as humanly possible, as my son breaks ranks from his graduation march to run up and plant a big, loud kiss on my cheek—*mmwwwaaa!*—and then run back to join his classmates. I'm laughing. I'm crying. I'm fine. I'm not fine. I have cancer. I'll deal with it. "Life changes in the instant. The ordinary instant," writes Didion (2005, p. 3).

The day after Sam's graduation, I returned to Massachusetts General, picked up my patient ID card, and had my pelvic MRI. Dr. Hong met with my husband and me soon afterward and gave us staggering news: On my medical records from Savannah, my tumor size was listed as 3.8 centimeters. A radiation plan had been put into place accordingly. At MGH, Dr. Hong's exam plus the pelvic MRI pegged the tumor size at 5.2 centimeters. The Savannah plan would not have been strong enough to eradicate the cancer. The chemo regime may have been the same, but the radiation was vastly different. I needed far more "aggressive" radiation. Before beginning treatment, however, Dr. Hong was going to let me heal. *Hallelujah!* Rather than beginning the following Tuesday, as Dr. Z. in Savannah had insisted, we would wait at least a week and a half, longer if necessary. "I want you healed up significantly, because once we start radiation, we aren't going to stop." *OK, fainting now.* Meanwhile, my husband would go back home to finish the last two weeks of school, and Sam would help me with my assignments for the next week: find a place to live, have the chemo port sewn into my chest, and attend orientation sessions for chemotherapy and radiation. There was no discussion about my returning home and coming back in a week or two. I could not bear to think of sitting on a plane for two more trips. I could barely sit in a cab for 10 minutes.

The brightest part of this golden option was that Sam had already planned to remain in Boston that summer, to study for the Bar Exam. This meant that I would get to see him far more often than I had in years. That fact alone would end up contributing more to my healing process than any drug or machine. Sam's presence there also allowed my husband to return home and wind up the school year. Again, providence seemed to have had a hand in the timing of this ordeal. My cherished husband Andreas, who would have to shoulder the burden of being "primary caregiver" for his cancer-patient wife, would be able to be at my side in Boston that summer with only a minimal amount of sick leave taken or "school business" to deal with.

By the time Andreas wound up the school year and came back up to Boston, I was installed in an apartment, knew the hospital like the back of my hand, and understood way more than any one person should ever have to know about 5-FU (Fluorouracil) and Mitomycin, my two chemotherapy drugs. (Later, I would tell the oncologist and chemo nurses, "Yeah, I've got 5-FUs for you . . .") The Mitomycin was administered in the chemo room on Day 1 of treatment, over a few hours' time. Then the 5-FU was inside of a pump, which was inside of a bag, which I had to carry with me like a purse, everywhere. A tube ran from the bag into the receiving port in my chest, bringing the chemo to me in a steady stream, 24 hours a day, for five days. (The process would be repeated four weeks later.) I slept with the bag, I took it into the bathroom, and it even hung by me while I took a shower or sat in my saltwater bath.

When I met the radiation nurse, she introduced herself by saying, "I'm Lorraine, and I'm going to be your BFF . . ." (Best Friend Forever). Lorraine was right. Radiation nurses rule the roost, as far as helping patients with the nuts and bolts of handling radiation burns. To this day I still email or call her with questions, and she answers immediately. BFF indeed! The actual radiation sessions involved "Big Blaster," a nickname I assigned to the mammoth machine used for roasting my behind. Since I had to face the machine *every day*, five days per week, for six weeks, Big Blaster became for me a personified, almost apologetic member of my medical team. This was the routine: A radiation technician, usually Jay, would help me up onto the table, where I would lie on my back and then awkwardly push my pants down to thigh-level. Jay would put a cushion under my knees (no fiberglass mold, no uncomfortable frog-legged position) and tell me to get comfortable. Looking at markers which were beamed down from the machine to my pelvis, Jay would adjust me one way or the other, so that the markers lined up with the tattooed dots on my pelvic and pubic bones.

CHAPTER 5

At that point I had to stop moving, so that the beams would stay right on target. Jay would go behind the wall and up a step to the observation window, start a Pandora station for music that would play over the speakers in the room, and then open his mic to say, "Hold still, Leslie." I would immediately freak out, worried that I would *not* be able to hold still. Seventeen minutes felt like infinity while lying rigid on a table. If I had coughed, sneezed, sobbed, or anything that would have caused even a slight movement (other than careful breathing) we'd have to start over, which would mean more radiation. Therefore, I forced myself to *hold still and breathe.* Big Blaster began his 360-degree coverage of me by first hovering directly overhead. He would then slowly move down and around until he was alongside of me, before disappearing under the table (somehow still blasting away at the tumor). Soon he would come up on the other side, peering at me again. He would go back up to hover over me once more, then repeat the circle, over and over, like an inquisitive alien, moving all on his own in a slow, methodical circle. Science fiction stories sometimes include aliens and anal probes. Instead, Big Blaster invaded my body with burning rays. The doctors were the ones who did the probing.

I fell into a routine of going to radiation every weekday, having my blood work drawn on Mondays, and having exams by Dr. Hong and Lorraine on Wednesdays. After that first week of being hooked up to the chemotherapy pump, I was very glad to have it removed. My hair began falling out right away. I found it all over the floor, the chairs, the kitchen counter, the pillows, and the bathtub. During my orientation, Dr. Kwak had predicted that I would not lose all of my hair, because it was very thick. She was right. It thinned out considerably and I soon had it cut short, but I did not go bald. If I had, I would have just gotten some big hoop earrings and rocked along, too concerned with the ultimate outcome to care about how I looked.

FORGET-ME-NOTS AND CONTRADICTORY SPACES

I was not a happy camper, by any means, but I was a confident patient. There was no more urge to flee. I was a patient being cared for by experts. One particularly magnificent way in which Massachusetts General cares for cancer patients is by providing exquisite Healing Gardens on the eighth floor of the cancer wing. Foucault (1967) wrote about heterotopias, or contradictory spaces that are "capable of juxtaposing in a single real place several spaces, several sites that are in themselves incompatible" (p. 6). The hospital buildings contained instruments of torture ("Big Blaster" and two treacherous chemotherapy drugs) used to destroy much inside me, yet those very same buildings were the spaces wherein *my cancer* would be eradicated, and where there were beautiful gardens directly on top of chemotherapy rooms—contradictory spaces indeed. What I find of particular interest is Foucault's (1967) third principle of heterotopia, where he speaks specifically of gardens:

> Perhaps the oldest example of these heterotopias that take the form of contradictory sites is the garden. . . . The traditional garden of the Persians

was a sacred space that was supposed to bring together inside its rectangle four parts representing the four parts of the world, with a space still more sacred than the others that were like an umbilicus, the navel of the world at its center (the basin and water fountain were there); and all the vegetation of the garden was supposed to come together in this space, in this sort of microcosm. . . . The garden is the smallest parcel of the world and then it is the totality of the world. The garden has been a sort of happy, universalizing heterotopia since the beginnings of antiquity (our modern zoological gardens spring from that source). (p. 6)

It may be hard to imagine being "happy" in the middle of cancer treatments, but the Healing Gardens made me happy, indeed. Andreas or Sam took me there any time I asked to go, and I asked often, even when I was at the point when I could only go by wheelchair. The gardens remind all who entered there that there is much splendor in the world, despite our experiences to the contrary. Patients, family members, and hospital staff go to the eighth floor to be transfixed by beauty. In the indoor garden there are stunning orchids, flourishing green plants, wicker chairs and couches with comfortable cushions, and peace. Conversation, if held at all, is carried on in hushed tones. With floor to ceiling windows, the indoor garden allows visitors to see the flowers, trees, sculptures, and the flat granite fountain outside. No one has to actually go outside to feel enveloped in tranquility, and soothed by nature.

Oh, but to go outside! That's what made me happiest, even though I was there in the middle of summer. (Boston summers are a breeze compared to southeast Georgia's heat and humidity.) Every time I went to the Healing Gardens, I had to get to that outdoor section. Since the hospital is located right across from the Charles River; I could sit by bushels of blue and yellow Forget-Me-Nots and stare at that river, watching sailboats and "Duck Tour" boats, for as long as I wanted. Patients undergoing chemotherapy have to be very cautious about the sun, avoiding it altogether. However, the trees provided shade, I was slathered in SPF, and I had a straw hat that stopped just short of being a sombrero. I couldn't stay long, but I just had to lay my eyes on those flowers, the fountain, and the sailboats. The Healing Gardens became, as Foucault (1967) termed it, my "sacred space" (p. 6). They were a vital component of my treatment regimen—a critical path toward my cure.

Contradictory spaces seemed to dominate my cancer treatments/cure. The gardens sat directly above the seventh-floor chemo rooms, where I had to sit while my body was being flooded with toxic chemicals—the rooms where they had to nearly kill us to cure us. The chemo room itself was a site incompatible with my wish to *not* feel the debilitating effects of chemotherapy drugs. Yet the room was compatible with my wish to kill the malignant tumor before it killed me. The gardens above were my haven, and yet, because of the pump, I had to bring the invasive chemo drug with me when I visited my sacred space during a chemo week. I had a similar love/hate experience with the radiation rooms, located in what I called the "Chamber of Horrors," deep down in the bowels of the hospital. There were times late in the

CHAPTER 5

treatment when I thought I could not climb back up on that table. However, putting a halt to the steady blasting of the tumor would have been disastrous. The radiation burns intensified over that summer across my backside, across my pelvis, and down my inner and outer thighs. Yet, radiation was the path to victory. I was being burned alive to remain alive. Radiation would ensure that I could stick around for a while. I had to embrace it, even though it made me cry. Often, I hurt, I couldn't help it. I also grieved. I grieved for my former self, my non-invaded-with-cancer self, which was gone for good. It was embarrassing how often tears came. I felt like more of a weakling, a "pansy," than ever before in my life. Joan Didion (2005), whose husband died of a sudden, massive heart attack, wrote:

> People in grief think a great deal about self-pity. We worry it, dread it, scourge our thinking for signs of it. We fear that our actions will reveal the condition tellingly described as "dwelling on it."
>
> The very language we use when we think about self-pity betrays the deep abhorrence in which we hold it: self-pity is *feeling sorry for yourself,* self-pity is *thumb-sucking,* self-pity is *boo hoo poor me,* self-pity is the condition in which those feeling sorry for themselves *indulge* or even *wallow.* (pp. 192–193)

I didn't want to wallow. I dreaded the self-pity, but I had a pretty large dose of it at times. Sometimes I cried right on the radiation table, even though I wasn't supposed to. I felt as though I had good reasons to do so. Although I couldn't sense the actual radiation waves at the time they hit me, I felt the *effects* of radiation more and more as time went on. The rays were targeting the tumor, which was *inside* of me, so my entire lower GI and urinary tracts were affected, in addition to all of the outside skin. The burns turned the skin on my entire backside and pelvic region varying colors as time went on: sunburn pink to serious-sunburn red to lightly-toasted brown to burnt-toast brown to nearly black. By the middle of the third week, I could not be stoic about the fact that every new turn on the table meant I'd be worse by the time I was trying to walk (or be wheeled) out of the Chamber.

Sometimes when I heard "Hold still, Leslie," the tears came before I knew what hit me. I wished I could control my emotions, but the tears were there, whether I wanted them to be or not. Prinze (2006) explains, "Once an emotion has been initiated, we cannot alter it by direct intervention. Initiation pathways and response pathways both operate without the luxury of control" (p. 236). I had to let the tears roll, hoping I wouldn't sob and thereby disturb Big Blaster's work. Each time I was helped off the table, Jay or another tech would pat me on the back and say, "You did great." I was a good girl; I held still. I didn't want to interrupt the radiation. I wear as a badge of honor the fact that never once did Jay have to come readjust me and begin again. My tattooed pinpoint dots stayed in line with the beams from Big Blaster perfectly. I needed Big Blaster to work.

On that dreaded table, I learned the art of holding still, as well as the art of *waiting. Waiting* for the session to be over. *Waiting* for the tumor to be gone. *Waiting* to get my life back. I had to hold my inner self still, as well—the more difficult endeavor, most of the time. To keep myself together, I would imagine (while *waiting*) how I might be different, post-cancer. I speculated about what it would feel like to not hurt anymore. I mused about what it would feel like to be cured. Eigen (2005c) discusses such *waiting*:

> One develops a holding environment for one's own being, a frame for waiting. Waiting on a feeling is not simply waiting a feeling out or putting oneself on hold, important as these are. To wait on a feeling allows reverie, imaginative reflection, a "feel" for oneself and one's situation, to grow. At the height of impossible struggle, one holds the self like a mother holds a baby. Holding as a prayer for development. (p. 175)

Holding still, Jay. Holding as a prayer for healing. Praying as a way of holding. Holding my body still. Holding my life still. Holding my fears in check, sometimes. Holding onto hope.

Once down from the table again, I would shuffle off to find my husband, who would take my arm (or help me to the wheelchair) and get me back to our temporary home: a rented apartment across the street from the hospital. My son found the place before treatments began, and although it cost a fortune to live there, the proximity to the Chamber of Horrors made the place ideal. I did not have to suffer through bumpy car trips to and from radiation each day, in Boston traffic, which I could not imagine enduring in addition to everything else.

The usual routine after returning from the hospital each morning was that I would go in the bedroom, shut the door, and lie down on the bed directly in front of a standing floor fan, with my housedress pushed up or pants pushed down, for an "an airing session." But I would then have to jump up and fly to the adjoining bathroom, because both chemo and radiation destroyed my GI tract. I tried to just *be still*, and *will* my intestinal tract to do the same. And then of course, there was the pain. I continued to have allergic reactions: closed-up throat, nausea, dizziness, hives—with all narcotics. Back when the biopsies were taken, the Savannah doctors and I thought we tried everything, pain medicine-wise. Those efforts paled in comparison to working with a palliative care specialist in Boston. Yet she could not help me, either. I'm curious about whether there is a psychosomatic component to this intolerance. My mother was not much of a pill-popper; alcohol was her drug of choice. I wonder if her addiction to alcohol makes me unconsciously fear becoming like her. Perhaps morphine would have worked for me if Jim Beam hadn't worked so well for Marcia for so many years. I would try to give myself a little pep talk: "This time, I won't get sick!" However, that was only wishful thinking. I always reacted to anything stronger than Advil. I had to deal with the pain on my own. End of story. My pain had its own story to tell. Prinze (2006) suggests:

> While pain is characteristically felt, pain involves more than feelings. Pain is the mind's way of registering physical pathology. . . . All pains carry the information about particular physical conditions. When we get distracted from

our pains while reading novels, the mind does not stop representing the state of the body. (p. 202)

I certainly tried to distract myself by reading. One would think that all the time spent in bed would be ideal for an avid reader. Books had been my avenues of escape as a child, and reading remained important to me forever more. However, the life-saving toxins in my system killed brain cells as well as tumor cells, making it impossible for me to read. (My body was the site of more contradictory spaces.) I had a classic case of "chemo brain." I'd heard the term before from my sister-in-law, Cindy, who had breast cancer. However, I thought that she made up the term. Unfortunately, chemo brain is very real. Patients who are affected by this disorder soon discover that their cognitive abilities become greatly diminished. There are also short-term memory problems, attention span issues, and difficulties with conversations (Mayo Clinic, 2010). My brain turned to mush.

Unable to read, I would just lie there in bed, staring at the window. The little TV in our rental apartment's bedroom did not have a remote, so it was hard to watch anything. I can't stand the increased volume used in commercials, but had no way to mute them. So the TV stayed off. I did watch a few DVDs on my laptop, eyeing them cockeyed from my side. I would fall asleep, wake up with a start, fly to the bathroom, then gingerly approach the bed again, trying not to sit directly on my behind as I returned to my side. Sleeping so much was exhausting, but I was so exhausted, I had to sleep. Recalling her own illness, Morris (2008) writes, "When one lives in the horizontal position one of the most important rhythms becomes sleep. Being ill means sleeping a lot. . . . I have never felt so weary, psychically and physically" (p. 74). *Weary.* Exactly.

When I was up for it, I could go get my "river fix." Another bonus to living near the hospital was that we were living across from the Charles River. In the late afternoon, Sam or Andreas would push me in the wheelchair, over the pedestrian bridge, down into the park nearby. I would watch the sailboats, and stop everyone who passed by with a dog to ask if I could say hello. Pet therapy to my heart's content—no wonder I was soon *cured.*

SO, WE WERE STUCK IN THIS PLASTIC, OUTDOOR ELEVATOR . . .

Mensch (2005) writes, "I have to return to the point that death does not illuminate itself. It casts its light on life" (pp. 169–170). In the midst of all the agonies of treatment, I chose to cling to my lifelong defense mechanism of choice: humor. (A friend who knows me well sent a tote bag printed with the message, "Cancer, you picked the wrong bitch." She knew I would treasure the bag more than teddy bears and lacey pillows.) As unlikely as it may seem, I was able to find some comical or absurd aspect of each day, which meant that I was able to be distracted for a moment, in the middle of cancer treatment hell. In her memoir, Carrie Fischer (2008) wrote, "I have to start by telling you that my entire existence could be summed up in one phrase. And that is: If my life wasn't funny it would just be true, and that is unacceptable" (p. 17). That is precisely how I felt. I returned to daily journaling, a practice that I had abandoned by the time I turned 16. This time around, I wrote for others, not just myself. Sharing the humorous moments that made my treatment period bearable developed into a task of primary importance for me.

CaringBridge, a remarkable organization that provides free web space for cancer patients' online journals, became my outlet and my chief method of staying in touch with family and friends while in Boston. Through CaringBridge, I was able to propel myself forward through the illness by, as Frank (1995) describes, "telling stories, specifically . . . 'self-stories.' The self-story is not told for the sake of description . . . the self is being *formed* in what is told" (p. 55) (emphasis in original). The *self* that I was forming was one who could cope with cancer the only way I knew how: by making fun of the situation.

Almost every day, something would happen that I'd truly find funny, and I'd write about it. I decided that I would go on record as making my illness story a humorous one whenever I could. Such was my method of interpreting, or, as Morris (2008) terms it, imagining my illness:

> The way one imagines one's illness has a great effect on coping with it. The way one imagines the illness also has a great effect on others. Being ill, means being ill in the context of the social. Illness happens in social webs. (p. 142)

During my 15 weeks in Boston ("summering in New England") I posted an entry almost every day. My written lines were my lifelines. I did not gloss over my misery from chemo and radiation; to the contrary, some who read the journal were put off by my very candid descriptions of what was going on with my body. It's just that I would also try to write about whatever I found humorous. I told myself that I was doing so primarily to make everyone else feel better about my situation. Soon, I realized that I wanted to make *myself* feel better. Anything that could lighten my day, or just a moment in my day, was a priceless diversion. Reacting with sarcasm and humor about trauma meant remaining within my lifelong comfort zone. I had been finding humor in the midst of wretched times since I can remember. Once my younger brother could talk, I had it made: a comic ally for life. As children and teenagers, we made fun of our situation to entertain ourselves, but we also tried to be funny for our mother, in order to entertain her. That was one way in which we tried to cope with her mood swings and depression, as Winnicott (1989a) describes. I was accustomed to looking around for something to find funny. Never was the search (*need*) for comic relief more urgent than when disease was wrecking my life. Writing during treatments helped me sling humor at the face of cancer.

Journaling was also a way of declaring to the world that I was still amongst the living, and was not going the way of Farah, or Jennie's dad. There I was, in the modern version of black and white: text posted on the web. *I chronicle, therefore I am.* As Frank (1995) explains:

> The act of telling is dual reaffirmation. Relationships with others are reaffirmed, and the self is reaffirmed. Serious illness requires both reaffirmations. . . . [T]

CHAPTER 5

he ill person needs to reaffirm that his story is worth listening to by others. He must also reaffirm that *he is still there*, as an audience for himself. (p. 56)

Many of my CaringBridge entries were posted while I stood up, typing at a laptop on a countertop. Sitting was not something I could do very easily while my backside was being torched. Leaning heavily to one side, putting my weight on one hip or the other worked, for short times, but it's hard to type while dangling over the edge of a recliner. Standing was best. I would sometimes stand rooted in one spot for over an hour, writing about the latest scary elevator encounter (my elevator karma was disturbingly off-kilter) or about the ridiculous complaint I made to a chemo nurse, when I insisted that the chemotherapy drugs were making my urine green (the culprit was blue toilet-bowl-cleaner in the tank). I recalled how my radiation technicians chose music for me based on requests from "other senior patients, like yourself." I described how a single strand of hair fell from my head, only to be blown by the air conditioning onto my arm while I was having radiation, making me think—with my south Georgia frame of reference—that one of those huge roaches was crawling on me. (I still think I deserve a trophy for not moving.) I didn't have to hunt for funny moments; they were everywhere.

When friends and family posted comments about looking forward to my next journal entry, I felt validated, and purposeful. I felt an obligation to keep going, be funny, and tell the truth about my illness. Certainly there were times when all I could post was "This is not a good day. Hope to write more soon." Usually, however, I could keep it up, and I continued to lay it on the line, most of the time. For example, I explained how especially severe the burns were along the "underwear line" on my legs, where the legs are hinged at the inner thigh. The burns were peeling (layers and layers) too soon, aggravated by my movements. Dr. Hong explained that the new skin was not "ready" to do its job as skin. It could not yet fill the role of outer layer of protection for the body. This reminded me of having terrible sunburn as a child, and pulling on the very edges of a spot that was beginning to peel, but pulling it back too far. Only, that feeling was magnified a thousand fold. I sat with frozen blueberries between my legs. My friends emailed links to me for stores specializing in women's boxers. A few sent huge housedresses, as big as tents, so that I could "go commando" (sans underwear). I definitely told it like it was, most of the time.

However, as graphic as I was about my burns and side effects, there were nevertheless many details that I left out. For all of my posturing about providing for future patients a totally straightforward account of the ordeal, I could not tell 100% of the story. There were indignities, and moments of pain and surrender that could not be shared, not even with my closest family members, not even admitted to myself. The *unsaid* hovered over my daily reports more and more often as treatment progressed. I wrote evasively, which meant a different sort of story was being told, as Peter Gay (1995) describes:

Diaries, precisely like their more coherent cousins, autobiographies, are all true, the evasive and mendacious ones no less than the others. They all testify, ingenuously or indirectly, to desires and anxieties, to pleasures and traumas, to inner discord discovered, at times fought out, pen in hand. (p. 344)

Still, I felt the pull to write an entry every time it was remotely possible. As Joe Kincheloe (1991) wrote, "Nothing ever happens once and is finished, the past lives on" (p. 130). Telling my story was my way of living on. Posting on Caringbridge kept me above water, if only barely.

At the worst point in the treatment period, I assigned to Dr. Hong a new name: "Dr. We-Don't-Stop-For-Skin," because that's what he would say to me every Wednesday when I'd try to make him agree with me that *this time, the burns are too severe to continue*. He would always tell me that his patients might have to stop treatments due to difficulties with chemotherapy side effects, but not for radiation burns. However, my body was rejecting the pain medicines that most patients take during radiation, so I couldn't even take the edge off the feeling of being scalded with branding irons, inside and out. I felt desperate. One time I said to my superhero doctor, "I really kind of hate you, you know." Adding insult to injury, by the fourth week of radiation, when it was time for the second round with the chemo pump, I was almost back in Geographic Cure, run-for-the-hills mode. The chemo destroyed my GI tract even more violently than it did during the first round. Such activity in the same area where severely burned skin was located meant agony. I wanted to tell Rosie the Riveter, "You are so wrong. I, for one, *cannot* do it."

However, if there was anything that could make me "pull up!" as Jacquelyn used to say, it was one good look around the radiation waiting room. There were *children* in there with me. Five-year-olds! Toddlers! If they could take it, what on earth was I doing feeling sorry for myself? I never heard a child say "No" when they were called back to their own Big Blaster rooms. Never did I see a child run the other way. Who was I, to think for a minute that I was dealing with "pain," when parents had to watch their *children* go through cancer treatment? Imagining what that type of pain would be like overwhelmed me. There was no comparison. I would be OK in the long run. I had no idea if those children would be, but I fervently hoped so.

Somehow, my inner Rosie hung in there all summer. The chemo did not destroy my heart or other major organs, and my cognition is back, mostly. Big Blaster (with his properly programmed strength for an accurately sized tumor) destroyed the growth, and two torturous chemotherapies made sure no stray cancer cells were able to regroup. Fleeing to Boston worked. I found a Geographic Cure. I wonder if the pattern I learned from my mother saved my life.

Boston remained my home for three additional weeks after the last radiation treatment. Even when I was finally released for travel, I wasn't sure I could sit on the plane long enough to get home. My friend Katherine came up to Boston to escort me back to Savannah, so that my husband could return to his teaching job on schedule. Sam was still in Boston, and saying goodbye to him nearly broke me in half. We had not spent that much time together since he left home for college. And when it came time to say goodbye to my medical team, I found that task more difficult than I expected. I was emotionally tied to them all. They saved me. Whereas in the middle of the summer, I wanted to ditch the lot of them and stop treatments altogether, by the end of August, tears of a different sort were springing up from nowhere. My farewell rounds were tough. Even Jay felt like a family member to me.

I was afraid of going so far away from my medical team, in order to go home. Although they'd said, "You're doing fine" all summer long in regard to the treatments themselves, there were major recovery issues that were not yet fine—not by a long shot. My radiation oncologist was the expert, and so was the radiation nurse. They knew how my burns would act while healing. I felt, perhaps unfairly, that there were no such experts back where I was going. I was flying from the nest, with no one in Savannah competent enough (in my opinion) with *my* cancer to catch me. This particular cure-seeking woman was not thrilled with returning to square one for recovery.

Fortunately, a safety net was installed. For two years, I returned to Boston every three months for follow-up care. The expense of all that travel was staggering. Yet, I'd go every month if that's what my team said to do, because every time I go, I ask Dr. Hong the same question: "Am I in remission, or am I actually cured?" He always answers, with total conviction: "You're *cured*." Blasting the tumor with an "aggressive" amount of radiation every day, five days per week, for six weeks without stopping . . . *that* was the plan. Running from treatment was not an option. I had to stay the course with Dr. We-Don't-Stop-For-Skin despite my inclinations otherwise at a few junctures. In the last two years of my mother's life, she battled a return of her breast cancer and ever-advancing, painful osteoporosis. She wanted to run, even though she would have needed someone else to carry her away. During what turned out to be her last month on earth, she talked about changing doctors and moving to a better place. I wonder if this is her legacy, that until I die, I'll be looking around for The Next Better Whatever in some form or other. Perhaps my inheritance from my mother saved my life.

HOLDING CHAOS AT BAY

When I began this book there was no thought to having a "cancer chapter." I revised my plan post-treatment, because the search for the Geographic Cure turned a much deeper shade of *literal* for me. This chapter is, as Frank (1995) terms it, my "quest story":

> Restitution stories attempt to outdistance mortality by rendering illness transitory. Chaos stories are sucked into the undertow of illness and the disasters that attend it. Quest stories meet suffering head on; they accept illness and seek to use it. Illness is the occasion of a journey that becomes a quest. . . . Though both restitution and chaos remain background voices when quest is foreground, the quest narrative speaks from the ill person's perspective and holds chaos at bay. (p. 115)

With any luck, perhaps my quest story will be heard by someone who has a nagging need to call a doctor. To that person I would say, here's the deal: I almost let procrastination (and embarrassment) kill me. I was *too busy* to go to a doctor, and too mortified. If we're pushing and pushing at work, and never letting up on ourselves (especially those of us who passed "middle age" a while ago . . .), what good will we be able to do for others when we start dropping like flies? And as far as losing all my dignity goes, "they" can have it. Over the span of just one summer, I dropped my pants for enough people (doctors, nurses, technicians, interns . . .) to fill Fenway Park. Dignity is overrated; to me, sticking around is the priority. Additionally, I hope my quest story might be heard by someone who worries about offending one doctor by jumping ship for another. Not every doctor can be an expert on every aspect of medicine, even within his or her own field. Personally, I chose to match my disease to a doctor's area of expertise. For my question, "How many times have you radiated someone's backside?" I wanted to hear an answer of "hundreds," not "four." I say, forget being loyal to the local tribe. I chased after the cure, and I jumped ship the minute I saw a more viable option. Cure-seeking behavior has its advantages.

At this writing, I have taken a giant step forward in the land of the cured. As mentioned above, for two years, I had been going back to Massachusetts General in Boston every three months for check-ups. But now I've graduated to a six-month schedule. For another two years at least, and maybe three, I'll return twice a year. After that, I'll only check in with MGH once a year. I love to say this out loud: I am not in remission, I am *cured*. I am active in the American Cancer Society's Relay for Life fund-raising efforts, and I speak to teams, volunteers, and supporters whenever I can, encouraging people to pay attention to their symptoms and to stop putting off colonoscopies or other unpleasant (or inconvenient) exams. I'll give my testimony about early detection and informed decisions to anyone who will listen, and now my written testimony is here for anyone who will read my story. Morris (2008) explains:

> The body is a social site of course, but when you are ill, you must become even more social via testimony. Testimony is an ethical, philosophical task. Testimony is also psychologically necessary. For without the telling of the tale in a way that speaks to others, falling forever into Hades becomes your fate. . . . Telling the tale might be a way to help someone else cope. There is no choice but to write and tell the tale. (p. 117)

By way of this chapter I am telling the tale, but I'm also asking some questions. What if chronic cure-seeking is "normal" for some people? What if it's normal for me? For instance, although I worked in the same school system for 28 years, I changed jobs within the system about every three to four years. Just because I've lived in the same house for two decades doesn't mean I've stopped chasing after that elusive Next Better. Conceivably, finding physicians with more experience justified my gigantic leap off the local medical community's ship. In reality, though, I admit that my *perception* of the local doctors' inability to heal me is what made me leave. Perhaps they would have been just as effective as the Boston doctors in

CHAPTER 5

saving my life. Maybe it was simply too late for Ken. If this is true, then did I run just for the sake of running, toward a perceived better place that caught my eye? If that's the case, this cure-seeking behavior makes me no different from my mother, or from the other cure-seeking people who have vexed my career life: the decision and policy makers in education who grab onto whatever trend or acronym catches their eye. Could it be that I do the very thing that I abhor?

Or . . . perhaps I am cured of the Geographic Cure. I didn't "run off" to Boston. I made an informed decision, and once I did so, I stuck with it. The decision to be treated there was not made on a whim, even though it was made quickly.

Perhaps there are times when a shift in direction, however radical or quickly turned, can be the difference between progress and stagnation, between life and death. Cure-seeking *must* have its place, then. Yet I have difficulties understanding the cure-seekers in education who frustrate me to no end. I'm leery of which leader's definition of "better" will be held up next as the light at the end of the tunnel. I'm weary of the constant chaos-producing changes that never allow teachers to just be left alone for a while. Through *currere*, I've come to understand this about myself: if change is all I know, then change is, potentially, my constant. Was change my mother's utopia? Bauman (2012) writes, "If a life of continuing and continuous hunting is another utopia, it is—contrary to the utopias of the past—a utopia *without an end*" (p. 108) (emphasis in original). That could be scary. If the Life Erratic is in my blood, then it might stand to reason that I will never stop hunting. Yet, there is the matter of informed decision-making, which is different from whimsy. Overall, I am a pretty solid person. I'm in my second marriage, but we are 23 years strong, and I am still crazy about my husband. My son Sam and my stepdaughter Colleen have known only one house as our family home. My close friends have been part of my life for decades. True, I changed jobs frequently within the same school system, but I didn't run away from education, even though the grass was greener on the "anywhere but here" side.

Self-examination is what leads me to consider these ideas. If only self-examination would be practiced by policy makers who steer the course of education according to which way the winds blow. The only "informed decisions" stem from bottom-line, business-model thinking. However, children are not products. They should not be used to garner profits. Head honchos in education who revel in data charts and "results" have agendas that collide with pedagogy. Borrowing from Bauman's idea, I call such head honchos "hunters." Sadly, it appears that the powers that be are only too happy to remain in continuous hunting mode. In my opinion, they create, for teachers, constant turmoil in their school environment. When I was in a central office position I saw for myself hundreds of teachers who are drained, overwhelmed, and overcome with feelings of defeat under the pressures from the hunters. *Hurry! Come this way! Don't go that way*—that was last year's direction!

Just as a young child *living* the Geographic Cure cannot tell a drunk parent to lay off (without fear of reprisal), teachers who are *working* the Life Erratic cannot tell the cure-chasing powers in education to lay off without fear of reprisal, either. My hope is that educators who are genuinely interested in the welfare of students may decide to overcome the threat of reprisal, and instead become vocal—calling on the hunters to give it a rest and leave teachers alone. Perhaps not forever, because thoughtful change can sometimes be a good thing. It would just be lovely if, for a while, the hunters who call the shots in education would just *hold still.*

CHAPTER 6

THE GEOGRAPHIC CURE WRIT LARGE

Ah yeah, you pay your fare
And if you don't know where you're going
any road will take you there
—George Harrison, *Any Road*

Unfortunately, in a classic version of bait and switch, the suggestions of governmental agencies are promulgated without the moral or financial support that would turn them into reality.
—Judith Remy Leder, *Whither Changing Schools?*
In *Traveller, Nomadic and Migrant Education*

Enduring clichés, like "walking a mile in someone else's shoes," also speak to the pedagogical importance of considering the world from the situation of another. While we have much information that speaks to why people feel separated from each other, we need more information about how people can learn to feel connected.
—Dan Chapman, *A Visual and Textual Analysis of Transnational Identity Formation and Representation*

Sometimes in education the frantic search for the Next Big Fix is as literal as my flight to Boston for a second opinion. For instance, in 2011, the Savannah newspaper reported on principal changes in the county school system that occurred between academic school years: "District officials aren't just modifying programs, replacing teachers and tweaking attendance zones as they cut costs and reform schools. They're shaking up school administration, too" (Few, 2011). That was the summer when 56 principals were reassigned before the school doors reopened in August. I was glad to see these changes made headlines, because I feel that the general public is unaware of the extent to which the Life Erratic occurs within schools.

I mentioned in Chapter 4 that a teacher can be that one person with whom a Geographic Cure Child might have a significant relationship (before he or she is carted off to the next school). I was not offering up some lofty, heartstring-tugging phrase for rhetorical effect. Time and again as I read studies on children being raised by alcoholic parents, I found that resilient Children of Alcoholics "had at least one person in their lives who accepted them unconditionally" (Werner & Johnson, 2004, p. 716). Today, I am nothing if not resilient, and I had several people who loved me unconditionally, including my poor, addicted mother (when she was sober). Since a few of the people I have in mind were teachers in the late 1960s and early 1970s,

CHAPTER 6

I try to imagine them teaching under today's conditions, yet having the time to listen to me, talk with me, and make me feel valued. I just can't imagine that happening. *There is no time.*

In the summer of 2012, I retired. There was no plan to do so until April. I "put in my papers" to end my career with the local school system at the end of the 2011–2012 school year. Friends and co-workers were startled to hear that I did this, because I am not yet 60 years old. I began this conversation about the Life Erratic, but then cancer interrupted me, like a rude party guest. I'm finishing my sentence now.

I graduated my doctoral program in December of 2012. I was often asked, "You won't get an increase in salary, so why are you bothering to get your degree *now*?" This question bubbles up from very same results-oriented cauldron that brews the Kool-Aid we're all expected to drink. The data-worshipping, "results" mindset is exactly what inspired me to complete my doctoral program, as well as this book. I have a passion, and I intend to be vocal about it. When I began in this field of curriculum studies, I was encouraged by Marla Morris to find my "voice." Why would I shut up now, just because I retired? I am beginning a conversation about children whose "home problems" amidst the Life Erratic are extraordinarily complex. I am moving Geographic Cure Children from the fringe into the center of teacher, counselor, and community health worker preparation programs. Awareness is only a first foray into understanding, but it's a vital one.

Curriculum theorists understand and refuse to minimize the fact that there is a *child* at that desk, not a means to an objectified end. In this field, alarm bells are sounding about the particular ends that drive those means above all others: "results," and, I assert, dollar signs. In schools, the *burden to produce* begets the *burden of neglect*. Teachers must produce "results" under accountability pressures of Adequate Yearly Progress, Pay-For-Performance, Race to the Top, and myriad other bribery tools (some meant to entice, others brazenly utilizing force) of the high-stakes results frenzy. This frenzy leaves teachers unable to even discover, let alone meet, children's needs. Teachers are not allowed to respond; they must instead make sure they are on the same page as everyone else on their grade level teaching the same subject. The bottom-line requirement for teachers is to *respond to what politicians need from the child:* score well, make us look good, help us bring high-end businesses and families (and wallets) to our states. Don't think. Don't consider the child. Just perform. As Pinar (2007) puts it:

> Educationally, such literalism takes the form of curriculum guides to be covered as if they were so many Internal Revenue Service (IRS) or Revenue Canada income tax regulations and procedures. Indeed, the curriculum is being audited. . . . This is anti-intellectualism at its most extreme, accountability covering up political manipulation and scapegoating. (p. 10)

Cloninger (2008) suggests that far too commonly, "our classrooms quash student participation and alienate students because of a lack of attentiveness, open-mindedness, and 'open-heartedness'" (p. 203). I've learned from hundreds of teachers, over nearly three decades, that in most cases, the issue is not a lack of genuine concern for children. The issue is that bottom line: *give us results, or find another job.* Children living the Life Erratic desperately need teachers to see them with open hearts, not exasperated bodies and minds. As Gouwens (2009) asserts:

> The children must feel that they belong in schools and classrooms, and they need to experience pedagogy that is relevant to them personally and culturally to be successful in school. They need teachers who are prepared to help them value their own cultural capital as well as to learn about, and come to value, the cultural capital of all of the children in the school. They need schools that are structured in ways that acknowledge and account for their travel and programs that help to prevent the gaps or to fill the gaps that occur while they are travelling. (pp. 221–224)

Certainly, it's important to think about ways to help all children feel that they belong in the classroom community. Yet, imagine the added difficulty in doing so for Geographic Cure Children who move so often!

The elusive quest for a cure on a larger scale traumatizes educators. Educational "leaders" (those pulling the reins, leading teachers and administrators around the pony circle) bombard educators with the New! Improved! way of doing everything—objectives, evaluations, curriculum "pacing," standardized tests—every year. It is absurdity, in my opinion; another ugly side of the Life Erratic with ramifications that strangle the creativity and warmth out of teachers across the globe. The more that education head honchos pile upon teachers, and the more they bully educators into working under the pressures of (increased!) standardization, accountability, and test-crazy schedules, the less likely a teacher will be to "lean in" to the Geographic Cure Child who arrives at the classroom door mid-year.

Yet that child *needs* that teacher! At school, that child needs to be welcomed, and valued, and that child needs to dwell in a peaceful environment for a few hours a day. To me, it is tragic that teachers who are stressed beyond their limits don't have time to care. I am joining the ranks of educators who speak out about this insanity. The completion of this book is not about an increase in pay. It's about considering my role in society: to think contrarily, and to read prudently, as Weaver (2010) calls for. I will continue to think differently, and will certainly continue this conversation.

Two decades ago, Phillip Jackson (1992) discussed the question of what university-based curriculum specialists actually *do*, and more specifically, what others think they "ought" to be doing. He wrote that there seemed to be two answers—one that is long established over the span of public education, and another that is yet to be fully articulated:

> The more recent answer . . . calls for the university-based specialist to be doing something different, something other than serving the practitioner's need for technical help in the arduous business of curriculum improvement and reform. . . . Another possibility is for them to bring to bear on educational matters

CHAPTER 6

in general the outlooks of scholarly disciplines and political perspectives that heretofore have been overlooked or largely ignored. (1992, p. 21)

Twenty years later, the field of Curriculum Studies is still doing "something different." This is why I am encouraged by my mentors and privileged to bring to this field a perspective that has been overlooked. I'm no specialist by any means. I have raised questions, but have not presumed to offer concrete answers. I certainly have not professed to know the Grand Fix, nor the Next Big Thing in Education. Even if cure-seeking behavior applies to us all at some point, to some degree, I still contend that such behavior runs *rampant* through most education policy-making circles, as erratically as it does in an 80-proof home. The *Next Better* remains frantically chased after in the wake of standardization, business-model schooling and accountability, and testing, testing, always more testing.

Susan Ohanian (2003) wrote a piercing criticism of "high stakes testing mania," brought on by the "Standardisto governors and their education minions" in their attempts to one-up each other in Adequate Yearly Progress (p. 736). Ohanian's article is ten years old now, and yet her point is timelier than ever: We are hurting children. It seems to me that education policy makers are addicted to the quest for a cure, in the sense that Bauman (2007) describes:

> As a means of quenching thirst, all addictions are self-destructive; they destroy the possibility of ever being satisfied.
>
> Examples and recipes remain attractive as long as they remain untested. But hardly any of them deliver on its promise—virtually every one stops short of the fulfillment it pledged to bring. (p. 72)

Bauman's description brings to mind the Greek mythological figure Tantalus. Poor Tantalus was doomed to stand in a pool of water from which he could never drink (when he bent down, the waters receded), and his thirst could never be quenched (Impelluso, 2008). The same can be said for many of those who brandish the power in education, looking for better "recipes" for success. These decision makers seem to be bowing and scraping at the feet of the be-all and end-all God of Test Results, clambering to continually change their "strategies" because *their* thirst is never quenched, either. Teachers and children pay dearly for this unending quest for the cure by the "parents" of schooling.

Marla Morris (2006) declares, "The standardized testing movement is horrifically anti-intellectual. It teaches children not to think. It teaches teachers not to teach" (p. 159). (I've seen cases where children have used teacher accountability pressures to their own advantage—"It's my teacher's fault if I don't score well." Parents jump on that bandwagon far too often as well.) All of the components of the standardization Teaberry Shuffle are rolled around like dice in a casino dealer's cup: they're tossed out, and what lands face up is what gets played for the moment. Then they all go back in the cup for the next roll. Veteran teachers tell newer teachers who balk at the revolving door of change, "This too shall pass. Something will be along to replace these new requirements soon enough." This is why I assert that teachers are *working a Life Erratic*.

I am relieved that curriculum scholars whom I admire have not walked away from the public school system in disgust. Teachers and children who are working and living without anchor have too few people in their corner. I feel that it's vitally important that educators in the field of curriculum studies keep these incredibly complex, critical conversations going. I'll keep them going with pre-service teachers, educators and administrators, members of the academy, and, especially, policy makers. I'm not "through," just because I retired from the public school system. I'm just getting started.

INSET: STEVIE, AGE 12

In the middle of a muggy late May morning, a seventh-grade boy named Stevie is called out of his English class by Ms. Bordino, a school administrator whom Stevie doesn't know. Ms. Bordino tells the young man, "Don't worry, son, you're not in trouble. I just need to run something by you. Come walk with me." She briskly walks past the noisy cafeteria on the way to the office. Stevie wonders how someone in high heels can walk so fast. (Ms. Bordino is dressed for success!) Along the hallway, the school's "data wall" shows the progress being made in every math class, on every grade level, for the entire middle school. Other hallways display data for other high-stakes subjects. Ms. Bordino and her appointed school-improvement team have been spending hours each week analyzing and discussing all of that data, in order to decide which areas of need will warrant the next big, school-wide, grade-level "push."

Ms. Bordino tries to make small talk with Stevie about the local minor league baseball team's recent victory, attempting to put the boy at ease. Stevie doesn't respond. He actually likes baseball, and his older brother Josh was briefly on a high school team. Josh made it to every practice and began the season as a relief pitcher, but then their mom decided they needed to move. Not too long after that, Josh turned 18 and moved out. Stevie doesn't feel inclined to talk baseball with this woman, who uses that familiar old *Fake Happy Voice*.

When they get to her office Ms. Bordino sits with Stevie at a conference table, and picks up a large brown file folder full of papers. There is lead in the air, upstaging the plug-in air freshener that shoots out a motion-activated fragrance (advertised as "calming" aromatherapy). Motivational posters, charts and graphs, and huge binders adorn the office walls and shelves. Stevie stares at the poster of an arrow that points to the words "Aim High and Shoot Straight! Keep Your Eye on Your Target!"

Ms. Bordino rifles through the folder, then begins the speech that Stevie knew was coming: "Steven, your school records were a mess to track down! Spartan Middle is your second school this year, and your 11th school since first grade? That has to be some kind of record!" She plasters a big smile across her face. Stevie shrugs. His stomach hurts badly, and his head is about to explode.

The administrator continues, "When your mother came to register you, back in January, we placed you in regular math because we assumed you could handle it.

CHAPTER 6

You have really been struggling in there, am I right?" Stevie stares at his shoes and barely nods.

"The scores for the state tests that you took earlier this month are back," Ms. Bordino continues, "and you scored below the minimum requirement in math. You'll have to take the test again on Monday. We need 100% of our re-takes to pass the second time around, so that we can get off the state's list of low-performing schools! You be sure to come to school on time for that re-take, OK?"

Stevie nods, knowing two things: (1) Mondays are bad days to expect his mother Kay to get him to school at all, let alone "in time" for anything. Yet he cannot take the school bus, because they are secretly living out of district. (2) He hates math because he doesn't *get* math. And taking that stupid test again will do nothing to his score. Stevie wonders if he will be the one to keep the school *on* that state list.

Ms. Bordino continues, "I know that we're about to end the school year, but I'm thinking about next year. Do you agree with me that you need *a lot* of help in math?" Stevie clutches his stomach and nods once again.

"I'd like to have you take more diagnostic tests on the computer in Mr. Robb's lab," Ms. Bordino said. "Just to give us some data—you know, information—about where you are . . ."

Stevie interrupts Ms. Bordino. "It doesn't matter where I am. I won't be here next year anyway, so just leave me alone!" His stomach clenches again, and he bolts up out of his chair. "I don't feel good. Can I go to the nurse?" Waterfalls threaten to tumble down Stevie's cheeks. He bends over slightly in acute pain.

Ms. Bordino writes out a hall pass and holds it out to Stevie. However, when he tries to take the pass, she latches on to the paper with a death grip. Glaring at him and speaking through a tightly clenched jaw, the administrator growls, "If you ever, *ever*, talk to me like that again, little man, I will have you in in-house suspension so fast your head will spin. I guess I need to call your mother and have a little chat with her." Only then does she release her grip on the hall pass. Stevie doesn't yell at Ms. Bordino, or kick a chair, or storm off. He simply takes the pass and walks out of the office. He cannot stand being growled at. He cannot stand being threatened. However, with the mention of Stevie's mother, fear jumped in and shoved anger out of the way. If Ms. Bordino tells Kay that Stevie said he won't be at Spartan next year, he will catch hell.

When Stevie goes to Ms. Canter, the nurse, she shuts the door behind him. "Stomach again, hon?" the nurse asks. He nods and angrily wipes tears from his face. "Come on over here and lie down." Certainly, the nurse's unfailingly calm and nurturing demeanor has been a balm to his tortured soul. But there's more. Stevie's school nurse has been the first informed supporter to recognize that he is a transient Child of an Alcoholic, living the Life Erratic, and this life is making him ill. Ms. Canter lets him stay there, on the cot, while she steps out to talk to the school counselor. Perhaps she and the counselor can put their heads together and figure something out. Stevie needs their help.

REFERENCES

Adger, Jr., H., Macdonald, D. I., & Wenger, S. (1999). Core competencies for involvement of health care providers in the care of children and adolescents in families affected by substance abuse. *Pediatrics*, 1083–1084.

Alcoholics Anonymous (AA). (n.d.). AA Glossary. Retrieved from http://www.ipass.net/a1idpirat/AAglossary.html.

Alcott, L. M. (1947). *Little women* (Junior Library ed.). New York, NY: Grosset & Dunlap. (Original work published in 1868.)

American Academy of Children and Adolescent Psychiatry (AACAP). (2011, March). Facts for families: Children and family moves. *American Academy of Children and Adolescent Psychiatry, 14*. Retrieved from http://www.aacap.org/galleries/FactsForFamilies/14_children_and_family_moves.pdf

American Academy of Child & Adolescent Psychiatry (AACAP). (2011, December). Facts for families: Children of alcoholics. *American Academy of Child & Adolescent Psychiatry, 17* Retrieved from http://www.aacap.org/publications/factsfam/alcoholc.htm

Anderson, W., Mendel, B. & Rudin, S. (Producers.) Anderson, W. (Director.) (2004.) *The life aquatic with Steve Zissou* [Motion picture]. United States: Touchstone Pictures

Aoki, T. T. (2005). Inspiriting the curriculum. In W. F. Pinar & R. L. Irwin (Eds.), *Curriculum in a new key: The collected works of Ted T. Aoki* (pp. 357–365). Mahwah, NJ: Lawrence Erlbaum.

Arman, J. F. (2000, April). A small group model for working with elementary school children of alcoholics. *Professional School Counseling, 3*(4), 290–293.

Artaud, A. (1988). *Antonin Artaud, selected writing*. Berkeley, CA: University of California Press.

Bainbridge, W. L. (2003, Saturday, May 24). Transient students are education dilemma. *The Columbus Dispatch*. Retrieved from http://www.schoolmatch.com/articles/cd2003May.htm

Ballard, M., & Cummings, M. E. (1990, June). Response to adults' angry behavior in children of alcoholic and nonalcoholic parents. *Journal of Genetic Psychology, 151*(2), 195–210.

Bartolomeo, C. (2006). When mom's a Marine. *NEA Today, 24*(6), 45.

Baudelaire, C. (2002). *On wine and hashish*. London: Hesperus Press. (Original work published in 1851.)

Bauman, Z. (2007). *Liquid modernity*. Malden, MA: Polity Press.

Bauman, Z. (2012). *Liquid times: Living in an age of uncertainty*. Cambridge, UK: Polity.

Benezet, A. (1774). *The mighty destroyer displayed: In some account of the dreadful habits made by the mistaken use as well as abuse of distilled spirituous liquors, by a lover of mankind*. Philadelphia, PA: Joseph Crukshank.

Bennett, L. A., Wolin, S. J., & Reiss, D. (1988, February). Cognitive, behavioral, and emotional problems among school-age children of alcoholic parents. *The American Journal of Psychiatry, 145*(2), 185–190.

Black, C. (1979, Fall). Children of alcoholics. *Alcohol, Health & Research World, 4*, 23–27.

Booth, M. (2008). *A brief history of opium*. Retrieved from http://www.opioids.com/timeline/

Britzman, D. P., & Pitt, A. J. (1996). Pedagogy and transference: Casting the past of learning into the presence of teaching. *Theory into Practice, 35*, 117–123.

Buber, M. (2004). *Between man and man*. New York, NY: Routledge.

Burnett, C. (2003). *One more time: A memoir*. New York, NY: Random House.

Burnett, G., Jones, R. A., Bliwise, N. G., & Ross, L. T. (2006). Family unpredictability, parental alcoholism, and the development of parentification. *The American Journal of Family Therapy, 34*, 181–189.

Burroughs, W. S. (2003). *Junky: 50th anniversary definitive edition*. New York, NY: Penguin Books. (Original work published in 1953.)

Carver, M. B. (2006). *What it used to be like: A portrait of my marriage to Raymond Carver*. New York, NY: St. Martin's Griffin.

Chao, R., & Clements, D. (2005). Studying homeless and highly mobile students at Westminster Elementary School: Raising awareness and building relationships. In Colorado Department of Education (Ed.), *Colorado Educators Study Homeless and Highly Mobile Students* (pp. 97–111). Denver, CO: Center for Research Strategies, Colorado Department of Education.

REFERENCES

Chapman, D. (2007). *A visual and textual analysis of transitional identify formation and representation* (Doctoral dissertation). Retrieved from http://www.libres.uncg.edu/ir/uncg/f/Chapman.pdf

Christensen, E. (1997, March). Aspects of a preventive approach to support children of alcoholics. *Child Abuse Review, 6*(1), 24–34.

Cloninger, K. (2008). Giving beyond care: An exploration of love in the classroom. *Curriculum and Teaching Dialogue, 10*(1 & 2), 193–211.

Cottle, T. J. (2004, Fall). Feeling scared. *Educational Horizons, 83*(1), 42–54.

Crespi, T. D., & Sabatelli, R. M. (1997, Summer). Children of alcoholics and adolescence: Individuation, development, and family systems. *Adolescence, 32*(126), 407–418.

Cuijpers, P. (2005, December). Prevention programmes for children of problem drinkers: A review. *Drugs, Education, Prevention, and Policy, 12*(6), 465–475.

Danaher, P. A., Kenny, M. & Leder, J. R. (Eds.), (2009). *Traveller, nomadic and migrant education.* New York, NY: Routledge.

Danziger, P., & Martin, A. M. (2000). *Snail mail no more.* New York: Scholastic Signature.

Darling-Hammond, L. (1998). Education for democracy. In W. Ayers & J. Miller (Eds.), *A light in dark times: Maxine Greene and the unfinished conversation* (pp. 78–91). New York, NY: Teachers College Press.

DeQuincey, T. (1998). *Confessions of an English opium eater and other writings.* New York, NY: Oxford University Press. (Original work published in 1821.)

Derrida, J. (2003). The rhetoric of drugs. In A. Alexander & M. S. Roberts (Eds.), *High culture: Reflections on addiction and modernity* (pp. 19–43). Albany, NY: State University of New York Press. (Original work published in 1990.)

Derrida, J., & Dufourmantelle, A. (2000). *Of hospitality: Anne Dufourmantelle invites Jacques Derrida to respond.* Stanford, CA: Stanford University Press.

Devine, C., & Braithwaite, V. (1993, January). The survival roles of children of alcoholics: Their measurement and validity. *Addiction, 88*(1), 69–78.

Dewey, J. (1997). *Experience & education* (1st Touchstone ed.). New York, NY: Touchstone. (Original work published in 1938.)

Dickson, P. (2009). *Drunk: The definitive drinker's dictionary.* Brooklyn, NY: Melville House.

Didion, J. (2005). *The year of magical thinking.* New York, NY: Alfred A. Knopf.

Doll, M. A. (2000). *Like letters in running water: A mythopoetics of curriculum.* Mahwah, NJ: Lawrence Erlbaum.

Doll, M. A. (2002). Portraits of anti-Semites. In M. Morris, & J. A. Weaver (Eds.), *Difficult memories: Talk in a (post) Holocaust era* (pp. 191–208). New York, NY: Peter Lang.

Doll, M. A. (2006). Shaping the stone. *English teaching: Practice and critique,* (2), 109–116. Retrieved from https://education.waikato.ac.nz/research/files/etpc/2006v5n2nar1.pdf

Doll, M. A. (2011). *The more of the myth: A pedagogy of diversion.* Rotterdam, The Netherlands: Sense.

Easley, M. J., & Epstein, N. (1991, April). Coping with stress in a family with an alcoholic parent. *Family Relations, 40*(2), 218–224.

Edwards, G. (2003). *Alcohol: The world's favorite drug.* New York, NY: St. Martin's Griffin.

Edwards, J. T. (1998). *Treating chemically dependent families: A practical system approach for professionals.* Center City, MN: Hazleden.

Eigen, M. (2005a). Afterword: The primitive background of experience. In A. Phillips (Ed.), *The electrified tightrope* (pp. 259–278). New York, NY: Karnac.

Eigen, M. (2005b). *Damaged bonds.* London, England: Karnac.

Eigen, M. (2005c). *Emotional storm.* Middletown, CT: Wesleyan University Press.

Eigen, M. (2009). *Flames from the unconscious: Trauma, madness and faith.* London, England: Karnac.

Felman, S. (1997). Psychoanalysis in education: Teaching terminable and interminable. In S. Todd (Ed.), *Learning desire: perspectives on pedagogy, culture, and the unsaid* (pp. 17–43). New York, NY: Routledge.

Few, J. (2011, July 17). 56 principals, 70 transfers: Savannah-Chatham school changes now a constant. *Savannah Morning News.* Retrieved from http://www.savannahnow.com

Fischer, C. (2008). *Wishful drinking.* New York, NY: Simon & Schuster.

REFERENCES

Flanigan, R. L. (2005). Great expectations. *American School Board Journal, 192*, 140–142.

Foon, D. (1993). *Skin and liars (two plays)*. Toronto, Canada: Playwrights Canada Press.

Forward, F., & Buck, C. (1989). *Toxic parents: Overcoming their hurtful legacy and reclaiming your life*. New York, NY: Bantam.

Foucalt, M. F. (1967). Of other spaces, heterotopias. Retrieved from http://foucault.info/documents/heteroTopia/foucault.heteroTopia.en.html

Frank, A. W. (1995). *The wounded storyteller: Body, illness and ethics*. Chicago, IL: University of Chicago Press.

Franke, T. M., Isken, J. A., & Parra, M. T. (2003, Winter). A pervasive school culture for the betterment of student outcomes: One school's approach to student mobility. *Journal of Negro Education, 72*(1), 150–157.

Freud, A. (1961). *The ego and the mechanisms of defense*. New York, NY: International Universities Press. (Original work published in 1936.)

Freud, S. (1969). *An outline of psychoanalysis*. New York, NY: W. W. Norton. (Original work published in 1940.)

Freud, S. (2003). The cocaine papers. In R. Shannonhouse (Ed.), *Under the influence: the literature of addiction* (pp. 25–34). New York, NY: Modern Library. (Original work published in 1884.)

Gallagher, T. (1992). *Moon crossing bridge*. St. Paul, MN: Graywolf Press.

Gance-Cleveland, B. (2004). Qualitative evaluation of school-based support group for adolescents with an addicted parent. *Nursing Research, 53*(6), 379–386.

Gance-Cleveland, B., Mays, M. Z., & Steffen, A. (2008, January). Association of adolescent physical and emotional health with perceived severity of parental substance abuse (Preview). *Journal for Specialists in Pediatric Nursing, 13*(1), 15–25.

Gantos, J. (2000). *Joey Pigza loses control*. New York, NY: Harper Trophy.

Garbarino, J. (2000). *Lost boys: Why our sons turn violent and how we can save them*. New York, NY: Anchor Books.

Garrison, J. (1997). *Dewey & eros: Wisdom & desire in the art of teaching*. New York, NY: Teachers College Press.

Gay, P. (1995). *The naked heart*. New York, NY: W. W. Norton.

Gibson, M. A., & Hidalgo, N. D. (2009). Bridges to success in high school for migrant youth. *Teachers College Record, 111*(3), 683–711.

Gouwens, J. A. (2009). Respondent's text. In P. A. Danaher, M. Kenny, & J. R. Leder (Eds.), *Traveller, nomadic and migrant education* (pp. 221–224). New York, NY: Routledge.

Grant, B. F. (2000, January). Estimates of US children exposed to alcohol abuse and dependence in the family. *American Journal of Public Health, 90*(1), 112–115.

Greene, M. (2001). *Variations on a blue guitar: The Lincoln Center Institute lectures on aesthetic education*. New York, NY: Teachers College Press.

Greene, M. (2009). Curriculum and Consciousness. In D. J. Flinders & S. J. Thornton (Eds.), *The curriculum studies reader* (pp. 155–167). New York, NY: Routledge.

Grostein, J. S. (1999). Humor and its relationship to the unconscious. In J. W. Barron (Ed.), *Humor and psyche: Psychoanalytic perspectives* (pp. 69–86). Hillsdale, NJ: The Analytic Press.

Gruber, K. J., & Taylor, M. F. (2006). A family perspective for substance abuse: Implications from the literature. In S. A. Straussner & C. H. Fewell (Eds.), *Impact of substance abuse on children and families: Research and practice implications* (1st ed., pp. 1–29). New York, NY: Routledge.

Grudin, R. (1982). *Time and the art of living*. New York, NY: Harper & Row.

Gruman, D. H., Harachi, T. W., Abbott, R. D., Catalano, R. F., & Fleming, C. B. (2008). Longitudinal effects of student mobility on three dimensions of elementary school engagement. *Child Development, 79*, 1833–1852.

Grumet, M. R. (2004). Word world: The literary reference for curriculum criticism. In W. F. Pinar (Ed.), *Contemporary curriculum discourses: Twenty years of JCT* (pp. 233–245). New York, NY: Peter Lang.

Grumet, M. R. (2006). Romantic research: Why we love to read. In G. M. Boldt & P. M. Salvio (Eds.), *Love's return: Psychoanalytic essays on childhood, teaching, and learning* (pp. 207–225). New York, NY: Routledge.

REFERENCES

Gunzerath, L., Hewitt, B. G., Li, T., & Warren, K. R. (2011, January). Alcohol research: past, present and future. *Annals of the New York Academy of Sciences, 1216*(1), 1–23.

Hagan, J., MacMillan, R., & Wheaton, B. (1996, June). New kid in town: Social capital and the life course effects of family migration on children. *American Sociological Review, 61*(3), 368–385.

Hall, C. W., & Webster, R. E. (2007, August). Multiple stressors and adjustment among adult children of alcoholics. *Addiction Research & Theory, 15*(4), 425–434.

Hall, T. (2001). Student movement. *Washington Monthly, 33*(9), 23–25.

Hango, D. W. (2006, November). The long-term effect of childhood residential mobility on educational attainment. *Sociological Quarterly, 47*(4), 631–664.

Hannon, L. (2009). *The cracker queen: A memoir of a jagged, joyful life.* New York, NY: Gotham Books.

Hardy, L. (2009). The changing face of homelessness. *American School Board Journal, 196*(6), 18–20.

Harrison, G. (2002). Any Road. [Recorded by G. Harrison]. On *Brainwashed* [DVD]. United Kingdom: Dark Horse/EMI.

Hart, K. E., & McAleer, M. (1997, December). Anger coping style in adult children of alcoholics. *Addiction Research, 5*(6), 473–485.

Haugland, B. S. (2005, April). Recurrent disruptions of rituals and routines in families with paternal alcohol abuse. *Family Relations, 54*(2), 225–241.

Helfenbein, Jr., R. J. (2006, Summer). Economies of identity: Cultural studies and a curriculum of making place. *Journal of Curriculum Theorizing, 22*(2), 87–100.

Hillman, J., & Ventura, M. (1993). *We've had 100 years of psychotherapy and the world's getting worse.* New York, NY: HarperCollins.

Huxley, A. (2004). *The doors of perception and heaven and hell.* New York, NY: HarperCollins Perennial. (Original work published in 1954.)

Hyde, C. R. (2007). *The year of my miraculous reappearance.* New York, NY: Knopf/Random House.

Impelluso, L. (2008). *Myths: Tales of the Greek and Roman gods.* New York, NY: Abrams.

Jackson, C. (1963). *The lost weekend.* New York, NY: Time.

Jackson, P. W. (1992). Conceptions of curriculum and curriculum specialists. In P. W. Jackson (Ed.), *Handbook of research on curriculum* (pp. 3–40). New York, NY: Macmillan.

Jacobson, L. J. (2001). Moving targets. *Education Week, 20*(29), 32–34.

James, W. (2008). *Talks to teachers on psychology and to students on some of life's ideals.* Champaign, IL: Book Jungle.

Jensen, A. (2009). Mobile children: Small captives of large structures? *Children & Society, 23*, 123–135.

Johnson, P. (2001, April). Dimensions of functioning in alcoholic and nonalcoholic families. *Journal of Mental Health Counseling, 23*(2), 127–136.

Keith, M. C. (2004). *The next better place: Memories of my misspent youth.* Chapel Hill, NC: Algonquin Books.

Kerbow, D. (1996). Patterns of urban student mobility and local school reform. *Journal of Education for Students Placed at Risk, 1*, 147–169.

Killeen, M. (1988). Self-concept of children of alcoholics: Part I. Family influences. *Journal of Child and Adolescent Psychiatric Nursing, 1*(1), 25–30.

Kincheloe, J. L. (1991). Willie Morris and the southern curriculum. In J. L. Kincheloe, & W. F. Pinar (Eds.), *Curriculum as social psychoanalysis: The significance of place* (pp. 123–154). Albany, NY: State University of New York Press.

Kirsch, A. (2005). *The wounded surgeon: Confession and transformation in six American poets.* New York, NY: W. W. Norton.

Kleinman, A. (1988). *The illness narratives: Suffering, healing and the human condition.* New York, NY: Basic Books.

Knelman, M. (2000). *Jim Carrey: The joker is wild.* Buffalo, NY: Firefly Books.

Knight, S. M., Vail-Smith, K., & Barnes, A. M. (1992, October). Children of alcoholics in the classroom: A survey of teacher perceptions and training needs. *Journal of School Health, 62*(8), 367–371.

Kullman, K. (2010, December). Transitional geographies: Making mobile children. *Social and Cultural Geography, 11*, 829–846.

REFERENCES

Lambie, G. W., & Sias, S. M. (2005, February). Children of alcoholics: Implications for professional school counseling. *Professional School Counseling, 8*(3), 266–273.

Lasch, A. A., & Kirkpatrick, S. L. (1990, November). A classroom perspective on student mobility. *The Elementary School Journal, 91*(2), 177–191.

Lasch, C. (1979). *A culture of narcissism: American life in an age of diminishing expectations*. New York, NY: W. W. Norton.

Lawson, C. A. (2004). *Understanding the borderline mother: Helping her children transcend the intense, unpredictable and volatile relationship*. New York, NY: Rowman & Littlefield.

Leder, J. R. (2009). Whither changing schools? In P. A. Danaher, M. Kenny, & J. R. Leder (Eds.), *Traveller, nomadic and migrant education* (pp. 214–220). New York, NY: Routledge.

Lender, M. E., & Martin, J. K. (1987). *Drinking in America: A history: The revised and expanded version*. New York, NY: The Free Press.

London, J. (1998). *John Barleycorn: 'Alcoholic memoirs'*. Oxford, England: Oxford University Press.

Lorde, A. (1997). *The cancer journals*. San Francisco, CA: Aunt Lute Books.

Lowry, M. (2007). *Under the volcano*. New York, NY: Harper Perennial. (Original work published 1947)

Lussier, K., Laventure, M., & Bertrand, K. (2010). Parenting and maternal substance addiction: Factors affecting utilization of child protective services. *Substance use and misuse, 45*, 1572–1588.

MacCready, R. M. (2006). *Buried*. New York, NY: Dutton Books.

MacDonald, A. (2004). *The way the crow flies*. New York, NY: Harper Perennial.

Marcus, A. M. (1986, March). Academic achievement in elementary school children of alcoholic mothers. *Journal of Child Psychology, 42*(2), 372–376.

Martusewicz, R. A. (2001). *Seeking passages: Post-structuralism, pedagogy, ethics*. New York, NY: Teachers College Press.

Maxwell, L. A. (2008). Student mobility in N.Y.C. *Education Week, 27*(32), 5.

Mayo Clinic. (2010) Chemo brain. Retrieved from http://www.mayoclinic.com/health/chemo-brain/DS01109

McDougall, J. (1985). *Theaters of the body: A psychoanalytic approach to psychosomatic illness*. New York, NY: W. W. Norton.

Menaker, E. (2001, March). Anna Freud's analysis by her father: The assault on the self. *Journal of Religion & Health, 40*(1), 89–96.

Mensch, J. R. (2005). *Hiddenness and alterity: Philosophical and literary sightings of the unseen*. Pittsburgh, PA: Duquesne University Press.

Middleton-Moz, J., & Dwindle, L. (1986). After the tears: Working through grief, loss, and depression with adult children of alcoholics. In R. J. Ackerman (Ed.), *Growing up in the shadow: Children of alcoholics* (pp. 225–234). Deerfield Beach, FL: Health Communications.

Milenkiewicz, M. (2005). Foreword. In *Colorado educators study homeless and highly mobile students* (pp. i–ii). Denver, CO: Center for Research Strategies, Colorado Department of Education.

Miller, A. (2005). *The body never lies*. New York, NY: W. W. Norton.

Miller, J. P. (1973). *The days of wine and roses: A play in three acts*. New York, NY: Dramatists Play Services.

Miller, P. M. (2009). Boundary spanning in homeless children's education notes from an emergent faculty role in Pittsburgh. *Educational Administration Quarterly, 45*, 616–630.

Million, J. (2000, November). Mobility matters. *PR Primer, National Association of Elementary School Principals*, 1–3. Retrieved from http://www.naesp.org/ContentLoad.do?contentId=229

Moorehouse, E. R., & Richards, T. (1986). An examination of dysfunctional latency age children of alcoholic parents and problems in intervention. In R. J. Ackerman (Ed.), *Growing up in the shadow: Children of alcoholics* (pp. 91–103). Deerfield Beach, FL: Health Communications.

Morris, M. (2001). *Curriculum and the Holocaust: Competing sites of memory and representation*. Mahwah, NJ: Lawrence Erlbaum.

Morris, M. (2006). *Jewish intellectuals and the university*. New York, NY: Palgrave MacMillan.

Morris, M. (2008). *Teaching through the ill body: A spiritual and aesthetic approach to pedagogy and illness*. Rotterdam, The Netherlands: Sense.

Morris, M. (2009). *On not being able to play: Scholars, musicians and the crisis of psyche*. Rotterdam, The Netherlands: Sense.

REFERENCES

Murray, B. L. (1998, December). Perceptions of adolescents living with parental alcoholism. *Journal of Psychiatric & Mental Health Nursing, 5*(6), 525–534.

Mylant, M., Ide, B., Cuevas, E., & Meehan, M. (2002, April). Adolescent children of alcoholics: Vulnerable or resilient? *Journal of the American Psychiatric Nurses Association, 8*(2), 57–64.

National Association for Children of Alcoholics (NACOA) (n.d.). Children of addicted parents: Important facts. Retrieved from http://www.nacoa.org

New Zealand Herald. (2005, December 21). Children suffering from frequent change of school. *The New Zealand Herald*. Retrieved from http://www.nzherald.co.nz/northland/news/article.cfm?l_id=139&objectid=10360960

Nissen, L. (2006, Winter). Curriculum and the geographic cure. *Journal of Curriculum Theorizing, 22*(4), 7–23.

Noddings, N. (1992). *The challenge to care in schools: An alternative approach to education*. New York, NY: Teachers College Press.

Nozik, M., & Wlodkowski, S. (Producers) & Jenkins, T. (Writer/Director). (1998). *The slums of Beverly Hills* [Motion picture]. U.S.: Fox Searchlight.

Offenberg, R. M. (2004). Inferring adequate yearly progress of schools from student achievement in highly mobile communities. *Journal of Education for Students Placed at Risk, 9*, 337–355.

Ohanian, S. (2003, June). Capitalism, calculus, and conscience. *Phi Delta Kappan, 84*(10), 736–747.

O'Rourke, K. (1990, December). Recapturing hope: Elementary school support groups for children of alcoholics. *Elementary School Guidance & Counseling, 25*(2), 107–115.

Padfield, P., & Cameron, G. (2009). Inclusion education for children and young people with interrupted learning in Scotland. In P. A. Danaher, M. Kenny, & J. R. Leder (Eds.), *Traveller, nomadic and migrant education* (pp. 29–46). New York, NY: Routledge.

Pagano, J. A. (2004). The curriculum field: Emergence of a discipline. In W. F. Pinar (Ed.), *Contemporary curriculum discourses: Twenty years of JCT* (pp. 82–105). New York, NY: Peter Lang.

Parks, M. (1999). Should we be working? In M. Morris, M. Doll, & W. F. Pinar (Eds.), *How we work* (pp. 263–273). New York, NY: Peter Lang.

Parsons, M. (2000). *The dove that returns, the dove that vanishes: Paradox and creativity in psychoanalysis*. London, England: Routledge.

Peleg-Oren, N., & Teichman, M. (2006). Young children of parents with substance abuse disorders (SUD): A review of the literature and implications for social work practice. In S. A. Straussner & C. H. Fewell (Eds.), *Impact of substance abuse on children and families: Research and implications* (pp. 49–61). Binghamton, NY: Haworth Press.

Phillips, A. (2001a). *Houdini's box: The art of escape*. New York, NY: Pantheon Books.

Phillips, A. (2001b). *Promises, promises: Essays on psychoanalysis and literature*. New York, NY: Basic Books.

Pinar, W. F. (2004). *What is curriculum theory?* Mahwah, NJ: Lawrence Erlbaum.

Pinar, W. F. (2007). *Intellectual advancement through disciplinarity: Verticality and horizontality in curriculum studies*. Rotterdam, The Netherlands: Sense.

Pinar, W. F. (2009). *The worldliness of a cosmopolitan education: Passionate lives in public service*. New York, NY: Routledge.

Pinar, W. F., & Grumet, M. R. (2006). *Toward a poor curriculum*. Troy, NY: Educators International Press.

Pinar, W. F., Reynolds, W. R., Slattery, P., & Taubman, P. M. (2002). *Understanding curriculum: An introduction of the study of historical and contemporary curriculum discourses*. New York, NY: Peter Lang.

Pitt, A. J. (2003). *The play of the personal: Psychoanalytic narratives of feminist education*. New York, NY: Peter Lang.

Plant, S. (2001). *Writing on drugs*. New York, NY: Picador.

Poe, E. A. (2003). The black cat. In R. Shannonhouse (Ed.), *Under the influence: The literature of addiction* (pp. 15–24). New York, NY: Modern Library. (Original work published in 1843.)

Post, P., & Robinson, B. E. (1998, June). School-age children of alcoholics and non-alcoholics: Their anxiety, self-esteem, and locus of control. *Professional School Counseling, 1*(5), 36–40.

REFERENCES

Powell, R. R., & Garcia, J. (1991, March/April). Classrooms under the influence: Adolescents and alcoholic parents. *Clearing House*, 275–278.

Price, H. (2006, July). Jumping on shadows: Catching the unconscious in the classroom. *Journal of Social Work Practice*, *20*, 145–161. http://dx.doi.org/10.1080/02650530600776830

Prinze, J. J. (2006). *Gut reactions: A perceptual theory of emotion*. New York, NY: Oxford University Press.

Prose, F. (2005, March 13). 'The glass castle': Outrageous misfortune. *The New York Times*. Retrieved from http://www.nytimes.com

Purpel, D. E. (2003). Foreword. In S. Books (Ed.), *Invisible children in the society and its schools* (pp. ix–xiii). Mahwah, NJ: Lawrence Erlbaum.

Robinson, B. E., & Rhoden, J. L. (1998). *Working with children of alcoholics: The practitioner's handbook*. Thousand Oaks, CA: Sage.

Roosa, M. W., Gensheimer, L. K., Short, J. L., Ayers, T. S., & Shell, R. (1989, July). A preventive intervention for children in alcoholic families: Results of a pilot study. *Family Relations*, *38*(3), 295–300.

Rorabaugh, W. J. (1981). *The alcoholic republic*. New York, NY: Oxford University Press.

Ruben, D. (2001). *Treating adult children of alcoholics: A behavioral approach*. San Diego, CA: Academic Press.

Sale, A. U. (2002). Drunk in front of the children. *Community Care*, 1433, 32–34.

Salvio, P. M. (2006). On the vicissitudes of love and hate: Anne Sexton's pedagogy. In G. M. Bolt, & P. M. Salvio (Eds.), *Love's return: Psychoanalytic essays on childhood, teaching, and learning* (pp. 65–86). New York, NY: Routledge.

Sanderson, D. R. (2003, March). Engaging highly transient students. *Education*, *123*(3), 600–605.

Schamp, J. (2002). Shadows from the inside out: The construction of memory as a space-between. In M. Morris, & J. A. Weaver (Eds.), *Difficult memories: Talk in a (post) Holocaust era* (pp. 69–104). New York, NY: Peter Lang.

Seixas, J. S., & Youcha, G. (1985). *Children of alcoholism: A survivor's manual*. New York, NY: Crown.

Sekoff, J. (2005). The undead: Necromancy and the inner world. In G. Kohon (Ed.), *The dead mother: The work of Anne Green* (pp. 109–127). New York, NY: Routledge.

Sher, L. (2006). Alcohol consumption and suicide. *QJM-An International Journal of Medicine*, *99*(1), 57–61. doi: 10.1093/qjmed/hci146

Shouting Inside. (n.d.). Whispers in the roar. Retrieved from http://www.shoutinginside.com

Slattery, P. (2006). *Curriculum development in the postmodern era* (2nd ed.). New York, NY: Routledge.

Smith, J. L., Fien, H., & Paine, S. C. (2008). When mobility disrupts learning. *Educational Leadership*, *65*(7), 59–63.

Steinberg, N. (2008). *Drunkard: A hard-drinking life*. New York, NY: Penguin Books.

Strand, S., & Demie, F. (2007). Pupil mobility, attainment, and progress in secondary school. *Educational Studies*, *33*, 313–331.

Supplee, A. (2004). *I almost love you, Eddie Clegg*. Atlanta, GA: Peachtree.

Thompson, S. H. (1998). Working with children of substance-abuse parents. *Young Children*, *53*(1), 34–37.

Times Educational Supplement. (2009, May 22). Scotland migrant numbers more than double. *Times Educational Supplement* p. 18.

Tinnfalt, A., Eriksson, C., & Brunnberg, E. (2011, April). Adolescent children of alcoholics on disclosure, support, and assessment of trustworthy adults. *Child and Adolescent Social Work Journal*, *28*(2), 133–151.

Torchia, M. M. (2003, August). Reaching out to children of alcoholic parents. *The Brown University Child and Adolescent Behavior Letter*, *19*, 1, 3–4.

Tyler, L. L. (1958, Winter). Psychoanalysis and curriculum theory. *The School Review*, *66*(4), 446–460.

Tyler, R. W. (1969). *Basic principles of curriculum and instruction*. Chicago, IL: University of Chicago Press.

U.S. Census Bureau. (2011). Census bureau reports housing is top reason people moved between 2009 and 2010. Retrieved from http://www.census.gov/newsroom/releases/archives/mobility_of_the_population/cb11-91.html

REFERENCES

U.S. Department of Health and Human Services Substance Abuse and Mental Health Services Administration (U.S. Dept. of HHS, SAMHSA) (1995). *What's important about children of alcoholics?* Retrieved from http://ncadi.samhsa.gov/govpubs/ph318/

U.S. Department of Health and Human Services Substance Abuse and Mental Health Services Administration (U.S. Dept. of HHS, SAMHSA) (2007, August 1). *Caring for kids whose parents abuse alcohol.* Retrieved from http://www.family.samhsa.gov/get/caringforkids.aspx

University of Pennsylvania Museum of Archaeology and Anthropology (UPMAA) (2008). *The origins and ancient history of wine.* Retrieved from http://www.museum.upenn.edu/new/exhibits/online

Veronie, L., & Fruehstorfer, D. (2001, Spring). Gender, birth order, and family role identification among adult children of alcoholics. *Current Psychology: Developmental, Learning, Personality, Social, 20*(1), 53–67.

Viadero, D. (2009). Out-of-school factors seen as key. *Education Week, 28*(24), 5.

Viorst, J. (1998). *Alexander, who's not (do you hear me? I mean it!) going to move.* New York, NY: Atheneum.

Walls, J. (2005). *The glass castle: A memoir.* New York, NY: Scribner.

Weaver, J. A. (2002). Silence of method. In M. Morris & J. A. Weaver (Eds.), *Difficult memories: Talk in a (post) holocaust era* (pp. 157–170). New York, NY: Peter Lang.

Weaver, J. A. (2010). *Educating the posthuman.* Rotterdam, The Netherlands: Sense.

Weiss, A. S. (2003). Baudelaire, Artaud and the aesthetics of intoxication. In A. A. Alexander & M. S. Roberts (Eds.), *High culture: Reflections on addiction and modernity* (pp. 157–171). Albany, NY: State University of New York Press.

Weissbourd, R. (1996). *The vulnerable child: What really hurts America's children and what we can do about it.* New York, NY: Perseus.

Wells, R. (1996). *Divine secrets of the ya-ya sisterhood.* New York, NY: Perennial.

Werner, E. E., & Johnson, J. L. (2004, April). The role of caring adults in the lives of children of alcoholics. *Substance Use and Misuse, 39*(5), 699–700.

Whitaker, M. (2006). Curriculum: Abuse or possibility? In M. A. Doll, D. Wear, & M. L. Whitaker (Eds.), *Triple takes on curricular worlds* (pp. 41–46). Albany, New York: State University of New York Press.

Windle, M. (1990). Temperament and personality attributes of children of alcoholics. In J. S. Searles & M. Windle (Eds.), *Children of alcoholics: Critical perspectives* (pp. 129–167). New York, NY: The Guilford Press.

Windle, M. (1996). Effect of parental drinking on adolescents. *Alcohol Health & Research World, 20*(3), 181–184.

Winnicott, D. W. (1989a). Development of the theme of the mother's unconscious as discovered in psycho-analytic practice. In C. Winnicott, R. Shepherd, & M. Davis (Eds.), *D. W. Winnicott: Psycho-analytic explorations* (pp. 247–250). Cambridge, MA: Harvard University Press.

Winnicott, D. W. (1989b). Ideas and definitions. In C. Winnicott, R. Shepherd, & M. Davis, *D. W. Winnicott: Psycho-analytic explorations* (pp. 43–44). Cambridge, MA: Harvard University Press.

Winnicott, D. W. (1989c). Psycho-neurosis in childhood. In C. Winnicott, R. Shepherd, & M. Davis (Eds.), *D. W. Winnicott: Psycho-analytic explorations* (pp. 247–250). Cambridge, MA: Harvard University Press.

Winnicott, D. W. (2004). *Playing and reality.* New York, NY: Brunner-Routledge.

Wood, D., Halfon, N., Scarlata, D., Newacheck, P., & Nessim, S. (1993, September 15). Impact of family relocation on children's growth, development, school function, and behavior. *Journal of the American Medical Association, 270*(11), 1334–1338.

Wurtzel, E. (2002). *More, now, again: A memoir of addiction.* New York, NY: Simon & Schuster.

Zehr, M. A. (2006). Migrant education. *Education Week, 26*(9), 16.

Zola, E. (2007). *L'Assommoir.* Champaign, IL: Book Jungle. (Original work published in 1877.)

CPSIA information can be obtained at www.ICGtesting.com
Printed in the USA
BVOW03s0030241013

334509BV00004B/112/P